HEMINGWAY'S SAINT LOUIS

How St. Louisans Shaped His Life and Legacy

by Andrew J. Theising
Initiative for Urban Research
Southern Illinois University Edwardsville

Edited by Bruce R. Olson
Author of *That St. Louis Thing* Vols. I and II

Cover design by Dallas Moses Design

Design and Production by LaVidaCo Communications

Published by and for:

Initiative for Urban Research
Southern Illinois University Edwardsville
Box 1453, Edwardsville IL 62026
www.siue.edu/iur

Images provided through the support and courtesy of:

- The Hemingway Foundation of Oak Park and the Oak Park Public Library, partners in the Illinois Digital Archives, Illinois Secretary of State's Office, Springfield, IL. <www.idaillinois.org>
- The Hemingway-Pfeiffer Museum and Education Center, Arkansas State University. Piggott, AR. <hemingway.astate.edu>
- The John F. Kennedy Presidential Library, Ernest Hemingway Collection. Boston, MA. <www.jfklibrary.org/archives/ernest-hemingway-collection>
- The Library of Congress, Historical American Building Survey, Creator, and Asa F. Tift. Tift-Hemingway House, 907 Whitehead Street, Key West, Monroe County, FL. Documentation: Compiled after [1933]. Photograph (public domain). Retrieved from <www.loc.gov/item/fl0149/>
- The National Archives and Records Administration, Passport Applications Files (databases used were acquired by the author's research collection). <www.nara.gov>
- Newspapers.com <www.newspapers.com>
- The University of Missouri Digital Library, Columbia, MO. <https://dl.mospace.umsystem.edu/mu/islandora/object/mu%3A5214>
- The Katharine Merrill Durand Family, Atlanta, GA.

The balance of the images were taken from material in the author's personal collection.

Cover Image: Ernest courting Hadley in St. Louis at 5739 Cates Avenue, probably May 1921. John F. Kennedy Library EHPH-05721.

ISBN: 978-1-950419-06-7

This book is dedicated to the memory of
Nancy June George (1963-2001),
who introduced me to the life of Ernest Hemingway over dinner in 1990.
See what you started?
Thirty years later, he is still the topic of conversation at the dinner table.

Ernest Hemingway.

Table of Contents

Introduction: All Roads Lead To St. Louis I

The Smith Family 1

The Richardson Family 31

The Pfeiffer Family 57

The Gellhorn Family 75

A. E. Hotchner and an Essay on Sources 99

Untimely Ends 114

Endnotes 115

Bibliography 135

Acknowledgements 139

Index 143

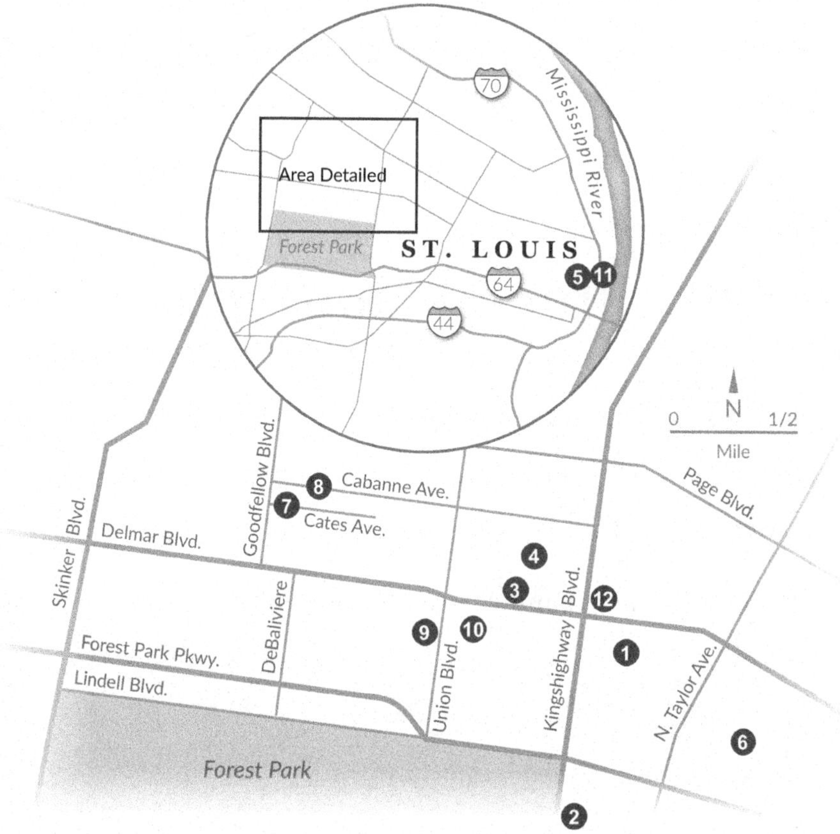

Smith family

1 Aunty Laura's home, where Ernest stayed (4748 Westminster Place)

2 Aunty Laura's apartment, where she died (14 North Kingshighway)

Pfeiffer family

3 Pauline Pfieffer's childhood home (5129 Delmar)

4 Gus Pfeiffer's 2nd home (5101 Kensington)

5 Allan-Pfeiffer Manufacturing Co., 1895 location (815 North 7th St. - Now America's Center site)

Gellhorn family

6 Martha Gellhorn's childhood home; where Ernest spent the night in May 1941 (4366 McPherson)

Richardson family

7 Hadley Richardson and Fonnie Usher's home, where Ernest stayed (5739 Cates Avenue)

8 Hadley Richardson's childhood home, where James died (5632 Cabanne Ave.)

9 Helen Pierce Breaker's childhood home (39 Kingsbury Place)

10 George and Helen Breaker's home, where the engagement party was held (5227 Westminster Place)

11 Richardson Drug Company - 1874 location on Laclede's Landing (704 1st Street)

A E Hotchner

12 1930s residence and setting for King of the Hill: Westgate Hotel (706 North Kingshighway)

Introduction: All Roads Lead To St. Louis

"...St. Louis affected me more deeply than any other environment has ever done.... I consider myself fortunate to have been born here...."

T. S. Eliot, in a letter to Marquis W. Childs

"I hate the place."

Tennessee Williams, to the Post-Dispatch

St. Louis is a literary city and always has been. Loved or despised, it has sent many of its daughters and sons into the world as contributors to human creativity: Maya Angelou, William S. Boroughs, T. S. Eliot, Sara Teasdale, Tennessee Williams, and the list goes on. Though Ernest Hemingway was not one of them, he was enabled in his craft by the goodwill of several St. Louisans.

Trumbull White, the seasoned journalist and retired magazine editor, gave Hemingway the best advice of his career during the summer of 1917: write about what you know from personal experience.[1] By then Hemingway knew he could write. Now he began to know what to *write about*.

Of all the people he met during these formative years when he became convinced he could be a writer, it was not the famous who were most important. His road to becoming an American literary giant was paved instead by those closest to him, beginning with Katy Smith, a St. Louis writer who introduced him to Hadley Richardson, her schoolmate also of St. Louis, and to her brother, Hemingway's closest friend Bill Smith. These were the people who started him on his way.

To describe Hemingway's presence in St. Louis would take only a few pages, but to describe the impact of St. Louisans on his life could fill volumes. His connections to the city are few but substantive. This monograph posits that many of the great adventures associated with him can be linked directly to the Gateway City. To be clear, this is not an argument that the city influenced his writing, but rather that its citizens influenced his experiences in magnificent ways and those experiences shaped his stories.

What are the great episodes of Hemingway's life? His expatriate years in Paris? Those were funded by first wife Hadley Richardson's trust fund that stemmed from the Richardson Drug Company of St. Louis. His first African hunting safari? That was funded through the generosity of second wife Pauline Pfeiffer's uncle Gus Pfeiffer and the Pfeiffer Chemical Company of St. Louis. His grand fishing expeditions in the Gulf Stream? Uncle Gus financed those too, though not the *Pilar*. How about his life at his Cuban estate, *Finca Vigia*? It was third wife Martha Gellhorn who found the property, fixed it up with her own money, and encouraged his move there. Even after his controversial death, his legacy was shaped by the first critical biography of Hemingway—compiled by his longtime friend and hometown boy A. E. Hotchner. The whole thing started with a childhood acquaintance with some older St. Louisans during the summer.

Indeed, Hemingway's career does not spring from the Chautauquas in upper Michigan or journalism mentors in Kansas City and Toronto, but rather with the Smith and Richardson families in St. Louis. Here then, for the first time together, is a close look at these St. Louisans whose indelible imprint was made on the life and work of Ernest Hemingway.

Lifelines

Life spans and marriages of Hemingway's wives

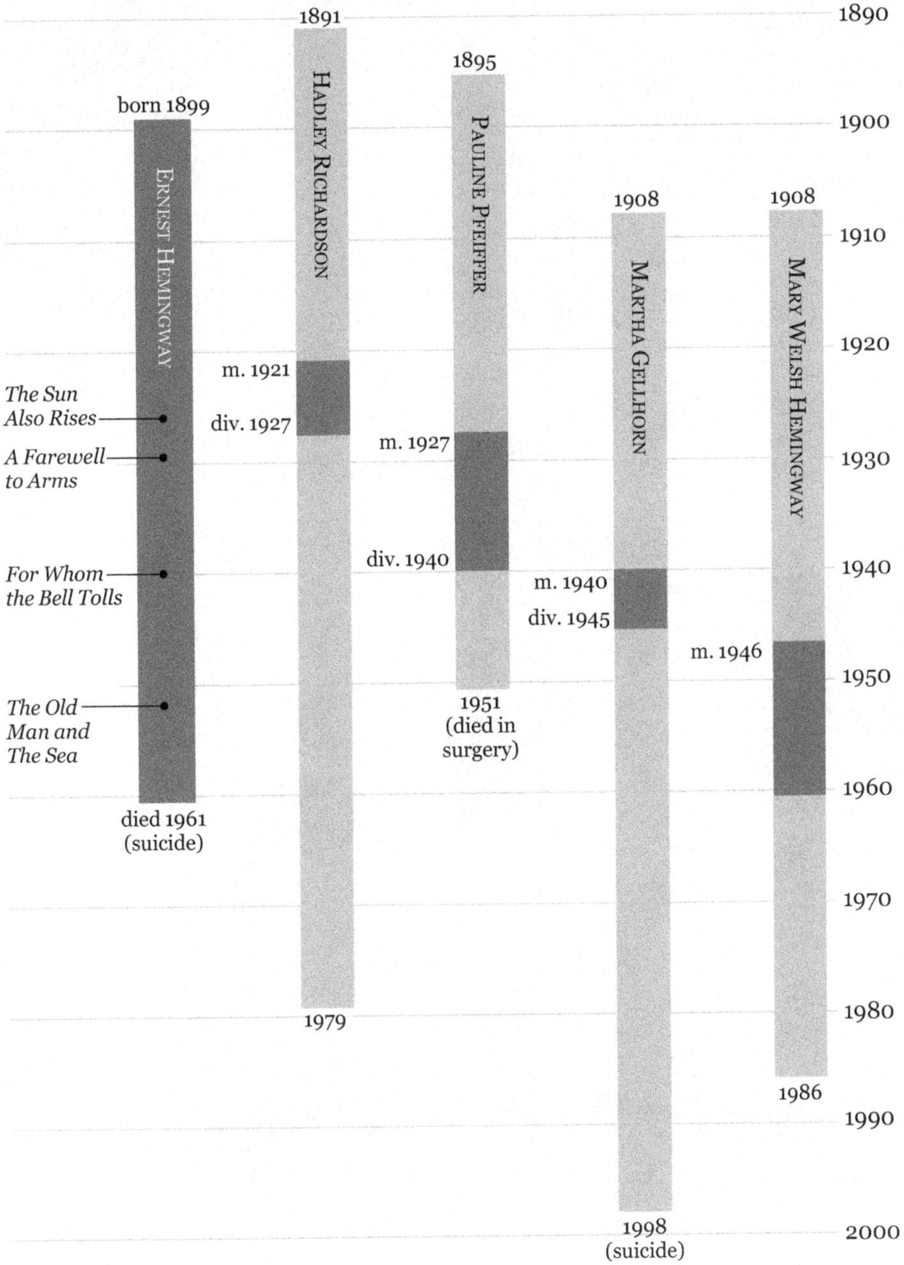

Laura Merrill Foster *(center) with nephew* ***Bill*** *(left) and niece* ***Katy*** *(right), about the time of her sister's death in 1899. Both of these children were born at Aunty Laura's home and left in her care while her ill sister sought treatment.*

The four children of Kate Merrill Smith, taken about the time of her death in 1899. From left: ***Merrill, Bill, Katy, Kenley****.*

K. M. Durand Family, public domain

1

The Smith Family

"Some may challenge the validity of this undertaking...but it is wrong to dismiss him."

Scott Donaldson's introduction,
By Force of Will

Katy's Two Moms: Mother Kate, Aunty Laura

The Smith children had a wild ride in life before they ever met Ernest Hemingway. Katy Smith was born October 26, 1891, in St. Louis.[1] She was a consumptive child, very likely because her mother was infected with tuberculosis during the pregnancy and would later die from it, probably passing the infection on to her newborn daughter.[2]

Katy's family was deep and rich. She was raised by her aunt, the prosperous Laura Charles (the former Laura Merrill), who provided her every luxury of the day. Not only did they give the security of decent housing, food, and family connection, she helped the young Katy weather the storm of her mother's early death.

One of the greatest gifts from Aunty Laura was enrollment in Mary Institute — a posh St. Louis girls' school founded by T. S. Eliot's grandfather William Greenleaf Eliot, who also founded Washington University in St. Louis. Hemingway's first wife, Hadley Richardson, knew Katy for eight years in school after meeting at age 11 when they were in the fourth grade, about the time Aunty was marrying Dr. Joseph Charles and establishing a new household in St. Louis.

Aunty Laura had brought a fortune into the family through her first husband, Gilbert Foster, a St. Louis businessman. He had been married previously to Catherine Mason, a daughter of one of the wealthiest and most powerful families in the United States. Mason was a descendant of the Duyckinck family—original settlers of New York City[3]—and related to the Delano, Roosevelt, and Tiffany families. Within months of that marriage the Mason heiress was dead. Gilbert Foster, 26, thus inherited both wealth and family. He moved into the house of his late wife's cousin, Isaac H. Knox (whose mother was a Mason).

Knox was the president of the St. Louis National Stock Yards in East St. Louis, Ill., and a Gilded Age magnate who operated in the circles of the Vanderbilts and J. P. Morgan. He gave his young cousin a job at the Stock Yards that led to a presidential appointment as Postmaster there from Grover Cleveland.

During the 1880s, Aunty Laura and Gilbert Foster rose to prominence in social circles. Though they easily could have afforded the opulent private streets of St. Louis, they did not live there. Instead, Gilbert and Laura resided across the river in East St. Louis, a rough-and-tumble town of industry and vice.[4] They lived on the site of the National Stock Yards in the National Hotel. While the hotel was somewhat removed from the livestock pens and slaughterhouses, it must have been difficult not to notice the surrounding air quality. Still, this was the family business and Gilbert was proud of his family's industrial empire. Gilbert died suddenly in 1894 at his residence there.[5] He was only 39. Aunty Laura inherited the whole of the Foster and Mason estates that had belonged to Gilbert, and continued to live at the National Hotel for at least two more years.[6]

Aunty Laura's brother, Leonard Merrill, was a real estate executive who established himself in St. Louis in 1884, and relocated to Los Angeles in 1892. He did quite well for himself in real estate there and later became a public official with the state. He invested his sister Laura's wealth, too, buying homes and ranches that would provide her income for years to come.[7]

Meanwhile, Kathleen[8] "Kate" Merrill (Katy's mother and Aunty Laura's sister) married Professor William Benjamin Smith in a big

Browne Photo, public domain

Left: The lovely ***Kate Merrill Smith****, mother of Merrill, Y.K., Katy, and Bill Smith. She may have been the first in the family to start spending summers in Michigan, where she died in 1899. Right:* ***Professor William Benjamin Smith Sr.*** *about 1890 when he would have been at the University of Missouri.*

Baptist church wedding in St. Louis in November 1882.[9] By the time baby Katy Smith came along in 1891 her mother was very sick from tuberculosis. She was mother Kate's third child, joining two older Smith brothers, Merrill and Kenley. A fourth child, Bill Jr., was born in 1895.

Kate contracted tuberculosis in 1890. She left her sons with her husband and sought a cure at various health resorts in New York, Colorado, Wisconsin, California, and Michigan.[10] While she was in Colorado Springs in 1891 she became pregnant with Katy, who was born at Aunty Laura's home. The baby was named Katharine Foster Smith, the middle name in honor of her sister Laura Merrill Foster. After the birth, Kate returned to Colorado Springs, followed the next summer by her sister Aunty Laura and little Katy.[11]

Before she became afflicted with TB, Kate enjoyed life abundantly. She was "a young woman of great personal charm and beauty, of high artistic nature, of high extraordinary gifts in singing."[12] She was singing in the grand opera at St. Louis by 1882 and was the lead soprano at the Church of the Messiah (where William Greenleaf Eliot had been founder and pastor), considered by many to have the best music in the city at the time.[13] Her hair was rich and golden, but her eyes were her most striking feature, described as "extraordinarily large and of a peculiar yellowish-green color" like that of a cat, which resulted in her nickname "Tabber."[14]

She remained close to her Merrill relatives, who lived in nearby Louisiana, Mo., a small town on the Mississippi River about 80 miles north of St. Louis. Her father was the town jeweler and ran his shop in the Bowman Building on Georgia Street in the heart of downtown. The society columns of St. Louis newspapers often tracked Kate and Laura's visits home to Louisiana, back to St. Louis, and off to other destinations. She took summers away, sometimes for pleasure and sometimes for health.

Michigan Summers with the Brothers and Sister Smith

Various members of the family had been going for years to northern Michigan to escape the summer heat of St. Louis. In 1896, Aunty Laura joined her cousin Jennie Drake Smith (a different Smith family from Kate's) to summer on Mackinac Island.[15] Laura took a liking to northern Michigan—perhaps for herself, perhaps for her sister.

Once she contracted tuberculosis, Kate's progress was up and down. She spent long months in a sanatorium and would recover some. She was deemed healthy enough in the summer of 1894 to return to her home in New Orleans where her husband was teaching.[16] No sooner had she settled back at home when Gilbert Foster died in St. Louis. The family was off to little Louisiana, Mo., where they marched over to the Riverview Cemetery and laid Gilbert to rest in the Merrill family plot. Kate became pregnant with her fourth child at the end of the year. Her son William Benjamin Smith Jr. was born in Aunty Laura's home on August 20, 1895, and he was left in Laura's care alongside his little sister Katy.

Things had been going fairly well for a time, perhaps long enough to think Kate was getting back to normal, but imagine

Laura's distress when she learned her dear sister was ill again. Kate was in New Orleans early in 1899. Perhaps the hot and humid South was not as nice a place to recover as the dry clean air of the Michigan peninsula. Perhaps Kate had been stricken for some time and was not healing under the living conditions of New Orleans. Perhaps Kate's husband, the professor, was too involved in his work at Tulane University to care for his ailing wife. Regardless of the reason, Laura stepped in and took charge.

Around Memorial Day 1899, Laura took her sister to Charlevoix, Michigan, not far from where Laura had vacationed on Mackinac Island. It is beautiful country on the shore of Lake Michigan.

Laura accompanied her sister and took the youngest children with her—her namesake niece Katharine Foster (now age 8) and her little nephew William Jr. (now age 4), who had been born in her residence at the National Hotel.[17]

Kate had secured a cottage at the Charlevoix Home Association property on the northwest edge of Lake Charlevoix.[18] She rented cottage #513 that hadn't been getting much use since its owner, Civil War General John H. King, died in 1888.

The Charlevoix Home Association operated a large resort assembled around the luxurious Belvedere Hotel. Cottages were built on wide tiers of land surrounded by water and forest. These "cottages" were affluent mansions with sweeping views and plenty of common ground for summertime activity.

The beer-loving Busch Family of St. Louis spent summers there until there was a formal objection to drinking alcohol on the front porch.[19] Kate had been a summer visitor to the Belvedere as early as 1887.[20]

However, Kate died of tuberculosis on June 12, 1899, only two weeks after being brought up north and just over a month before Ernest Hemingway was born.

Her husband and the older boys were on their way from New Orleans, having been wired earlier. All the family members, north and south, took the train to little Louisiana, Mo., and marched over to the Riverview Cemetery, where Kate was laid to rest near her father.

In an arrangement that suited Professor Smith just fine, Aunty Laura kept little Katy and Bill, and the Professor kept the two older sons, Merrill, 16, and Kenley, 13.[21]

In 1901, Laura made her regular summer trip to Michigan. She stopped in Petoskey, a railroad center that received trains from Chicago and St. Louis, and served the nearby towns like Charlevoix and Horton Bay.

She booked time at the Roaring Brook Inn at Harbor Springs, perhaps because she had young kids in tow, perhaps because the old cottage was not yet ready for long occupancy, or perhaps the memories of Charlevoix were still too fresh and they needed to try someplace new.

The newspaper reported that there were 104 people from St. Louis and Chicago on that train, and one of those St. Louisans making the trip was Dr. Joseph W. Charles, an eye doctor who had been trained in America and Europe—and he was single.[22]

Perhaps they met on the train. It was a long journey from St. Louis to Petoskey and there was plenty of time for two people to get to know each other. Surely, Aunty Laura and Dr. Charles crossed paths at the Inn throughout summer vacation. Laura's widowed mother was living with her and made the trip too.[23] Somewhere that summer, a courtship began.

Laura Merrill Foster and Dr. Joseph W. Charles were married the following spring in 1902. They married in Aunty Laura's St. Louis home at 4459 Delmar Boulevard, with Dr. Charles's father, the Reverend Doctor Benjamin Hynes Charles, officiating.[24]

Aunty Laura bought cottage #513 at the Charlevoix Home Association in 1903. She held on to it for more than a dozen years, waiting for the tragic memories to fade.[25]

In 1913, Aunty Laura bought a farm property that came up for sale across Lake Charlevoix on a nook called Horton Bay. The farm had an old house sitting atop a hill surrounded by an orchard, with woods in the back and the waters of the bay visible from the front. Horton Creek flowed along the property's edge and was full of trout. The front porch was bare, but there was a garage in back, as well as a chicken coop.[26] The farm on Pincherry Road had been the home of Alonzo J. Stroud, whose family operated the sawmill in the small town—one of the earliest businesses there.

Katy Captivates Young Ernest

Around the time Kate died, in 1899, Dr. Clarence and Grace Hall Hemingway purchased the old Bacon place on Walloon Lake, a smaller body of water adjacent to gigantic Lake Charlevoix. In 1900, they built a cottage there that Grace named Windemere.

Ernest Hemingway first engaged the Smiths meaningfully in 1916 as a 17-year-old high school student. Starting that year, when he began hanging out with the Smiths and the other summer people, Ernest found his friends' company to be "so gay and witty and so ready to share," he saw it as a new channel for meaning in his life.[27]

Katy Smith was 25 and brother Bill Jr. was 21 when they met Hemingway. Another Michigan friend was Carl Edgar who was older still, aged 27. These ages may be surprising to those familiar with the Hemingway lore of joyful teenage summers in northern Michigan. These friends of Ernest's youth were not peers playing on vacation from school. In reality, these were career-minded men and women who were already living independent lives.

Ernest was the laggard. His father hoped that these older acquaintances would have a "steadying influence" on

Ernest Miller Hemingway's *high school graduation photo, May 1917. He was a high school student when he started hanging out with much older companions in Horton Bay.*

Ernest Hemingway Foundation of Oak Park, through Illinois Digital Archives MHS349-0006-1261

Katy Smith's *portrait in the 1913 University of Missouri Savitar, representing her class in the University Women.*

University of Missouri Library, public domain

John F. Kennedy Library EH05529P

***The "summer people"** in Michigan, about 1920: from left, Carl Edgar, Katy Smith, Marcelline Hemingway, Bill Horne, Ernest Hemingway, Bill Smith. Ernest points his pistol at the camera.*

the boy.[28] Little did he know how powerful these influences would be. Biographer Mary Dearborn notes that Ernest's intelligence and wit set him apart from his age group, and that this helped him be accepted by his older companions.[29]

Katy, his first St. Louis woman, would prove fascinating to Ernest and if she wasn't his first true love, she came close. Much has been written about Katy's appearance, especially her eyes. Hemingway biographer Carlos Baker described her as "neither quite pretty nor quite plain, an outspoken girl with flyaway hair...always brushing it out of her eyes with the back of her slender hand."[30]

Like her mother, her eyes "were green as a cat's" and were her most "arresting feature"—making you think she could "see in dark."[31] Her eyes must have been mesmerizing. In examining the published photos of her from over the years, she rarely looks at the camera.

It may be too much to say that Katy was in love with Ernest Hemingway. If that were the case, there were many chances for an independent woman like Katy to have seized the opportunity with a teenage boy. However, it seems certain that Katy indeed saw Ernest as a viable option for a life partner and was reluctant to surrender that choice (right up to the last moments before his marriage). Maybe she didn't want Ernest until she couldn't have him.

Despite their age difference, they were close, they were flirty, they enjoyed each other's company in Horton Bay and later in Chicago, where their friendship became year-round. There were many people keen on Katy, though, and Katy enjoyed the single carefree life.[32]

There was speculation of a physical relationship between Katy and Ernest early in 1921. She certainly was a love interest of Ernest's in the years after he came back from World War I and before he left for Paris.

There is also speculation about Katy's bisexuality. According to neighbors during her early years in Provincetown, she was part of a "lesbian enclave." She was living there with her longtime friend Edith Foley in a cooperative housing arrangement that also included her brother Bill called "Smooley Hall" (the name being a combination of its members Smith, [Stella] Roof, and Foley).[33]

Katy Smith worked as a writer doing magazine features, ad copy, and some fiction. She published fiction under pseudonyms like "Katharine Carr"—for she knew Aunty Laura and her professor father would not approve of her subject matter.[34]

She and Edith were the first of the group to move to Provincetown (after 1921), soon to be followed by the rest of the Smooley gang. Her brother Bill, at the time, was still dividing his time between St. Louis and Horton Bay, while also making a jaunt to Europe.[35] By summer of 1924, they were all on Cape Cod.

Ernest Hemingway, of course, never married Katy Smith but she introduced him to the woman he would marry: her high school friend Hadley Richardson. But they continued their friendship through the years and across marriages, including in 1929 when she married Ernest's friend and colleague John Dos Passos. Here Ernest introduced Katy to her husband, just as Katy had introduced Ernest to his wife. Katy was killed in an automobile accident in 1947.

By then, Hemingway and Katy had fallen apart, particularly over the offense Katy took at Ernest's treatment of his second wife. Ernest's dislike of Katy was cemented for him in 1951, when Dos Passos released *Chosen Country*, a book that portrayed a Hemingway-esque character unfavorably. Katy was dead by then but details in the book could only have come from her.

Bill Smith's wife Marion Hammett said Katy hated Ernest in the end because of his treatment of Pauline Pfieffer, his second St. Louis wife (third St. Louis woman if you count Katy herself). Ernest

John F. Kennedy Library EH01515

***John Dos Passos** (1896-1970) reads to his wife, **Katy Smith Dos Passos**, 1932. Carlos Baker described her as "neither quite pretty nor quite plain, an outspoken girl with flyaway hair ... always brushing it out of her eyes with the back of her slender hand." They supposedly met at Ernest's Key West home and married in 1929. She was five years older than him and lied about her age.*

had hurt Katy's high-school friend Hadley, and now had treated her college-friend Pauline badly by being unfaithful and belligerent.

Katy is not buried in Louisiana, Mo., next to her mother and ancestors. Instead, Eben Given, another man who had a crush on her at one time, arranged her burial hastily. He had her buried in his family plot near the ocean at Snow Cemetery on Cape Cod.[36] Dos Passos, who remarried and survived Katy by many years, is buried with his second wife.

The Gentry of Horton Bay

By 1913, the old Stroud place on Horton Bay became known as Charles Farm, and Aunty Laura by then was called "Aunty Charles" or, as Ernest would call her, "The Madame." She ruled the roost up in Michigan.[37] Katy was then in her 20s and soon would be living in Chicago with her older brother Kenley. Her younger brother, Bill Jr., was about to enroll at the University of Missouri to study agriculture.

Aunty Charles, whom Bill Smith said was never in very good health,[38] died in her St. Louis apartment on March 31, 1924, at the age of 64 of a heart ailment. Once again, the family boarded a train to little Louisiana, Mo., and marched over to the Riverview Cemetery. They laid the matriarch of the family to rest, near to her sister Kate, her father, and at the feet of her first husband Gilbert Foster. Her grave is marked with only a small granite brick with her initials—nothing else. It is an understated remembrance of a woman who lived so large.

Aunty Charles did not think highly of young Ernest. In fact, Bill Smith said he did not like young Ernest either but was persuaded by Carl Edgar to give Ernest a chance. Other Horton Bay families had similar negative attitudes about Ernest, too. Everyone liked the Hemingway parents but Ernest did not seem to live up to their reputation.[39]

Ernest did not like "The Madame" and told his friend Howell Jenkins that Bill Smith could take his whole family and jam it up an elephant's ass. Ernest put his anger into a 1922 poem where he called Aunty Charles a drooling bitch and her home a house of lies.[40]

Nonetheless the Madame and the Doctor, the Charleses, were the gentry of Horton Bay. Each June, the family would make the train trek up to Michigan. When they arrived at the Petoskey station, they would be chauffeured to Charles Farm by the finest auto in town, which was Lester Fox's fine brass-trimmed Ford.[41]

The town of Horton Bay sits near the very top of lower Michigan about 175 miles north of Grand Rapids and some 100 miles from the Canadian border. The little town (2010 pop. 500) sits between the eastern shore of giant Lake Charlevoix and the western shore of smaller Walloon Lake.

K. M. Durand Family/James Durand

Picnic at Charlevoix, c. 1902. "The cross is Aunty," is written in Bill's hand on the back. ***Aunty Laura*** *looks as if she's holding court.* ***Katy*** *is seated to Aunty's left. Young* ***Bill*** *stands at center with hands behind his back. Teenager* ***Merrill*** *sits in profile in checkered pants. Teenager* ***Kenley****, with his dark hair, is seated behind his brother.* ***Professor Smith*** *is seated at the rear of the photo, admiring an unidentified girl.*

Here was a general store, the Dilworth family rental cottages and restaurant, the Methodist Church, and the historic mill. The actual water feature called Horton Bay is in Lake Charlevoix, formed by a sandy "point" where Horton Creek drains into the lake. Charles Farm was on the lake where the creek meets the bay.

The Hemingway cottage Windemere was built on the eastern shore of Walloon Lake. In 1905, the Hemingways bought the Longfield Farm property on the western shore of Walloon Lake, on the wide strip of land between Walloon and Charlevoix. It was just a couple miles from the town of Horton Bay and not far from Charles Farm.

In 1916, the Smiths of Charles Farm started engaging the young Ernest Hemingway at the Dilworth Inn. They undoubtedly crossed paths before but it was at this time most historians agree that they all started spending time together.

Neglectful, Disliked, Lauded Dr. Smith

Missing from Michigan was Kate's husband, the Smith family father, Dr. William Benjamin Smith, Ph.D., LL.D. He was a mathematician and philosopher who lived for his work. He started his career at Central College in Fayette, Mo., (now Central Methodist University) and later taught at the University of Missouri in Columbia. He spent the bulk of his career, however, teaching at Tulane in New Orleans, where he was chair of mathematics in 1893 and then was given a professor position in the philosophy department in 1907.

When he died, the University of Missouri produced a memorial essay exalting the man, comparing his brilliance to Kant, saying his intellect was equal to Goethe, and placing his scholarship on the level of Leibniz.[42] He met Kate Merrill in Fayette where Kate was teaching piano and vocals at Howard Payne College.[43]

Professor Smith's academic record was striking. He completed his degrees early. He was a department chair early in his career and was successful as an administrator. He tangled with some university presidents but was still asked to deliver the commencement address — drawing even more accolades.[44] He published works in English and German, in mathematics and philosophy, and was working on a new translation of *The Iliad* at the time of his death.

1850–1934

Dr. William B. Smith

Educator Dead At Age of 83

Columbia, Mo.—(AP)—Dr. William Benjamin Smith, professor emeritus of philosophy and mathematics at Tulane University, died yesterday in his 84th year after a 4-day illness.

Newspapers.com; public domain

Death notice of Professor ***William B. Smith Sr.****, 1934 showing the professor in regalia. He was buried in Louisiana, MO next to his wife. Y.K. and Katy gave their shares of the estate to their brother Bill, whose career had not blossomed like theirs.*

There was another side to the professor's scholarship, however. He wrote some controversial books beginning in 1894, arguing that the origins of Christianity were in a pre-Christian Jesus cult centuries before Jesus appeared in any human form. And in 1905 he published a book that argued that whites were genetically superior to Negroes.[45] In 1912, after studying new census data, the predicted African Americans would be extinct from the United States in 2123.[46]

His children remained divided from him after his wife's death and Professor Smith seemingly gave no resistance to the plan. He was devoted to his work and always had been.

Aunty Charles didn't like him. Bill Smith said his Aunty Charles felt Professor Smith neglected his family, especially his sick wife. Aunty Charles blamed him for her sister's death, or at least hastening it.[47] Walter Miller, a lifelong friend and colleague of Professor Smith, said that Professor Smith had utter disdain for

Aunty Charles, a woman Miller described as "Satan incarnate."[48] Thus, Professor Smith was not welcome at Charles Farm and rarely visited. When he did, he stayed at the Dilworth Inn rather than at the farm with the Charles family.

Hemingway biographer James Mellow tells a story of Professor Smith that illustrates his disinterest in his family. According to family lore, the second of the professor's sons, Kenley, and his friends had been staying at Charles Farm and were floating on Lake Charlevoix when a storm came up. Aunty Charles began to worry for their safety, found the professor, and insisted he do something.

The professor put down his studies for a moment and then walked to the shore of Horton Bay. He looked for the group out on the water and yelled, "Oh Lord, give up Thy dead." He then left and returned to his study.[49]

Professor Smith retired from Tulane in 1915. He received a meaningful pension as an emeritus professor ($2,400 annually, or $60,000 today) and moved back to central Missouri where he spent the rest of his life. [50] His family scattered, he was taken in by the Everman family of Columbia.[51] Curtis Everman admired Smith and felt for a man who was "lonely" yet "courteous" and with "great personal charm."[52]

He died August 6, 1934. Katy and Kenley were with him, as were members of the Everman family. The published cause of death was heat exhaustion, but he had underlying heart problems that were exacerbated by his age. He was now 83 and enduring the extreme heat of the Dust Bowl era. His obituary appeared in *The New York Times* and extolled his academic record of eight books in multiple languages.[53]

Once again, the family took the train to Louisiana, Mo., and made the march over to Riverview Cemetery to fill another grave in the family plot. Though his will divided his estate among his three surviving children, Katy and Kenley gave the estate to their brother Bill.[54] Bill and Kenley sponsored a posthumous publication of their father's ninth work, *The Birth of the Gospel* in 1954.[55]

Bill Jr.: Drunken Pal in Life and Literature

National Archives and Records Administration; Theising Collection

***Bill Smith's** passport photo from 1925, using his inheritance from Aunty Charles to visit Ernest in Europe. He was recently released from the sanatorium. His career was flagging while his siblings enjoyed rising success. Hemingway described him on that trip as being despondent and even suicidal.*

The professor's youngest son, Bill Jr., probably was Ernest's closest male friend during the Michigan years and into later life. Their friendship was slow to start but was meant to last despite Ernest's various outbursts and condemnations. In Michigan, young Bill had the nickname "WeeJun," and it was Bill who gave Ernest the lasting nickname "Wemedge," and perhaps taught Ernest a love for giving nicknames.[56]

Bill was born in East St. Louis and raised in St. Louis by Aunty Charles. Like his mother and sister, he also had bouts with tuberculosis—and it may have been present at his birth just as was with Katy. His childhood, also like Katy's, was rather idyllic and the children wanted for nothing materially.

Bill made the regular trips to Michigan with Aunty Charles, even after Katy was independent of the household. Though Bill moved around St. Louis as a young adult, he always was based out of the Charles family home.

In St. Louis he lived with Hadley's family on Cates Avenue and on nearby Waterman Avenue. Various St. Louis city directories list him as a salesman for Mid-States Motors at 2646-48 Locust Street, a job that allowed him the summers in Michigan he craved.[57]

One of the St. Louis homes he and his aunt shared was at 4748 Westminster Place. The Charleses had purchased the house late in 1920 from the Miller family whose daughter, Patsy Ruth Miller, became a Hollywood starlet, appearing opposite Lon Chaney in *Hunchback of Notre Dame* (1923).[58] The Doctor's brother lived just down the street at #4711.[59] In May of 1923, Aunty Charles and The Doctor downsized (probably due to Aunty's deteriorating health) and moved to the Bellevue apartments at 14 N. Kingshighway, overlooking Forest Park.

Later, after Hemingway left for Europe, Bill Smith tried his hand at writing short stories, inspired by his visits with Ernest in Paris and Pamplona. He gave up, though, and eventually took a job

Left: The home of Aunty Charles at ***4748 Westminster Place*** *in St. Louis. Ernest stayed in this home on his first visit to St. Louis when courting Hadley, March 11-13, 1921.*

Right: The lovely Bellevue Apartments, ***14 North Kingshighway Boulevard*** *in St. Louis, where Aunty Charles died in 1924. It is the second in a row of four identical buildings with names beginning A-B-C-D.*

Theising photos

writing for government publications arranged by mutual Hemingway friend Harold Loeb. It was while working for Loeb that he met his wife Marion Hammett.[60]

When he visited Paris in 1925, Ernest described him as "despondent" and even "suicidal."[61] Smith's visit distracted Ernest from his writing, but Ernest said Bill had been "a wonderful guy."[62] As Ernest's and Katy's lives seemed on the rise, Bill's seemed flagging. He spent the balance of his career as a public servant in various federal agencies. The highlight of his career was writing portions of speeches given President Harry Truman.[63]

Bill Jr., like Ernest, was an alcoholic.[64] The two men bonded over drinking and the outdoors. Bill had an appreciation of Ernest's pride in strength, youthful ebullience, and ability to spin yarns.[65]

Ernest remembered Bill in his writing, telling stories of their drinking at Charles Farm in "The Three Day Blow."[66] During the dry days of Prohibition, Bill made home brews popular among his friends.[67] The character Bill Gorton in *The Sun Also Rises* largely is based on Bill Smith, and Smith acknowledged (with pride) that the drunkenness of the character was a trait taken from him.[68]

He and his wife Marion lived in New York and later Arlington, Va. Bill died on Jan. 25, 1972, at age 76. He is buried in Hollywood, Florida. His wife donated his Hemingway papers to Princeton University. The scholar Donald St. John did an excellent interview of Bill in 1968, and published a considerable number of photos that do not appear in the usual Hemingway sources. Marion was a primary source for Virginia Spencer Carr's thorough biography of John Dos Passos (and his wife, Katy Smith). Coincidentally, at the time of this writing, Bill Smith's treasured version of *For Whom the Bell Tolls*, given to Smith by the author and signed "Wemedge," was put up for auction.[69]

Y.K.'s *Mad Men* Life in Chicago

The connection between the Smiths and Hemingway was made stronger by Katy and Bill's older brother, Kenley (called Kenley professionally but called by his initials Y.K. among family and friends). When the children were split up, he stayed with his father in New Orleans. By 1920 he was established in Chicago and would prove to be a valuable

Newspapers.com; public domain

***Y. K. Smith** press photo. He was the advertising man at whose Chicago home Ernest met authors, artists, and Hadley. His mistress tried to kill him in 1924. He married three times.*

facilitator for Hemingway's St. Louis connections.

Of the whole family, it is Y.K. Smith who received the strangest name—and it should be no surprise the name came from his professor-father. The first name was Yeremya, a corruption of Jeremiah, Professor Smith's father's name. The odd spelling was because of Professor Smith's scholarly disdain for the letter "J," an alphabet "interloper" unknown to Latin or Greek, and true scholars (like himself) used "Y" instead. Kenley was the professor's mother's maiden name.[70]

According to the Griffin biography of Hemingway, Y.K. lived in St. Louis until 1919.[71] In Chicago he lived with his sister Katy and other summer people. His WWI draft card gives an address in Syracuse, N.Y., perhaps a temporary address while he was being treated for TB at the Trudeau Sanatorium in Saranac.[72] (Bill Smith's WWI officer training application came from Horton Bay.)

Y.K. loved to be around artists and, in Chicago, worked successfully in advertising, starting with the firm Critchfield's.[73] One almost needs to envision the television series *Mad Men* (starring St. Louis-born actor Jon Hamm) to appreciate the money and lifestyle of advertising executives in the mid-20th century, a lifestyle that very much suited the hard-drinking Y.K.

His "wife" (perhaps a common-law wife rather than a formally-betrothed bride) was Blanche Genevieve Dawley Smith—a.k.a. "Doodles" or later "Vieva." They had met at the tuberculosis sanatorium. Regardless of the formality of their relationship, it appeared to be an open marriage.

Y.K. rented a "palatial" apartment (Hadley's word) at 63 East Division Street[74] in Chicago that had at least seven rooms. One of the spaces was rented to his sister Katy and her friend Edith Foley. Another was rented to Don Wright, Y.K.'s co-worker and friend who flirted with Doodles in ways that pointed to an affair.

The apartment was a clubhouse for Chicago artists, rooms filled with friends and creative souls whom Y.K. admired. One of these rooms would soon belong to Ernest Hemingway. When the tenant Hemingway criticized the way Y.K. let Doodles treat him, Y.K. became furious and Ernest wound up sleeping on the roof.[75]

Y.K. was involved in a strange affair in 1924 that drew national media attention. In 1922, he met a young lawyer named Wanda Elaine Stopa, whom he thought had great artistic potential. She was said to be the "youngest and first woman assistant U.S. Attorney in Chicago history."[76] This claim may be an exaggeration but there is no doubting that she and Katy's brother had a life-altering relationship.

He saw her as a promising writer and agreed to subsidize her at $150 per month (about $2,200 today) [77] so she could move to New York and pursue her talent. She gave up her life and career in Chicago and began writing stories. But the talent apparently was not as deep as Y.K. thought and the stories went unpublished.

By 1924, Stopa (age 24) became obsessed with her benefactor (age 37). Perhaps Y.K. had sent her away to end the affair between them. She thought Y.K. was about to break up with Doodles and would be free to marry her.

She had meanwhile married a Russian count, but was planning to leave him for Y.K. She wrote letters to Y.K., fantasizing what this next phase of life for them would look like. Y.K. completely disengaged from her and quit sending the monthly stipend. Stopa was distraught.

She decided she would kill him. She sent him a box of chocolates laced with poison. She watched the newspapers for an announcement of his death, but saw nothing. She telephoned him, saying she was coming to Chicago. Wanda took a cab from Chicago's Union Station to the suburb of Palos Park, where the Smiths were living. She entered the house but Y.K. wasn't home.

Instead, she found Doodles. Wanda blasted Doodles verbally with a barrage of complaints and accusations. Her yelling was heard by the gardener, Henry Manning. The 68-year-old Manning ran to help just at the moment Wanda drew a pistol and aimed it at Doodles. She wasn't bluffing with the gun, but proved to be as good a shot as she was a romance writer. Four shots rang out. Three missed entirely, but the fourth killed Manning instantly.[78]

Wanda calmly left the house, went back to her waiting cab, and caught a train to Detroit. Once there she checked into a room at the Hotel Statler. She sat down and wrote a long letter to her mother, then swallowed a poison pill. As soon as she sensed the poison taking effect, she picked up the phone and told the operator to send a doctor because she was not feeling well. Her body was found a few minutes later.

The newspapers were in flames over the story. "Good Girl Gone Bad," shouted the *Chicago Tribune*. "Wandering Wanda" recounted another. Thousands of curiosity-seekers lined her funeral route and mobbed the streets around the church where the service was held.[79]

Y.K.'s marriage to Doodles ended thanks to the Stopa affair.[80]

Ernest's summer gang was short-lived. The first to go was Y.K. himself, after Ernest wrote a vicious letter to him. Eventually, Ernest would reject the whole group—Bill Smith (who would later come back), John Dos Passos (and with him, Katy), Sherwood Anderson, and even Hadley.

Bill Smith always denied that there was a falling out, it was just a "falling apart" over distance and time.[81] There may be confusion, said Bill, with the falling out that Y.K. and Ernest had. This is a charitable remembrance by Bill, since Ernest fired off at least one angry letter to Bill, and Bill wrote back that he sided with his brother Y.K. in the matter, and that he and his family did not like the "1922 edition of Ernest Hemingway" but hoped for better.[82] Bill Smith did resume his relationship with Ernest a few years later.

Y.K. married second wife Julia in 1942 and moved to New York. After her death, he married a third time to the former Helen Asbury (Mrs. Herbert Asbury).[83] He died in 1969, age 83.

Family on the Fringe

Another fixture in the Michigan scene was Aunty Charles' husband The Doctor, Dr. Joseph W. Charles, whom Bill Jr. called "Unk." Bill's recollection of Unk was not as sharp as that of his

DR. JOSEPH W. CHARLES

DR. JOSEPH W. CHARLES, EYE SPECIALIST, DIES

Ophthalmologist Here for 54

Newspapers.com; public domain

Death notice for ***Dr. Joseph W. Charles****, 1950. He remarried after Aunty Charles died and lived another 25 years. There is no evidence that he ever returned to Michigan or maintained any relationship with the Smith children.*

Aunty Laura Charles. Joseph is described as being busy and away most of the time. This is consistent with the social calendar announcements in the newspaper—Aunty Charles and family were on their way north, and Dr. Charles would join them later.

Bill also recalled meeting the fiery preacher that was Unk Charles's father—the Reverend Dr. Benjamin Hynes Charles, who had been a pastor at Presbyterian churches in Clayton and St. Louis. Bill recalled how he would slap the table with his cane three times to emphasize the three components of the Holy Trinity.[84] The Reverend Charles died in 1914.

The Doctor may not have approved of Ernest, and Ernest did not fully approve of him, but they got along enough to play tennis together in the summer of 1920.[85] Dr. Charles seemed to have a passion for the sport. Ernest did not like the fact that Dr. Charles wanted to be referred to by the title "doctor." This may be due to Ernest's misunderstanding of his specialty.

Dr. Joseph William Charles was not an optometrist as has been attributed,[86] but in fact was a fully-trained and accomplished ophthalmologist, and perhaps one of the leading ones in Missouri. He served on the faculty of the St. Louis University School of Medicine and also at Washington University in St. Louis. The Governor of Missouri appointed him a trustee of the Missouri School for the Blind and he was invited to be a Fellow of the American Medical Association.

He was a member of several other professional societies dedicated to the study of the eyes. He earned every bit of the title "doctor." It seems unusual that the son of a physician would not understand or value that. To be sure, some of Ernest's disdain for Aunty Charles must have rubbed off on The Doctor.[87]

Dr. Charles was an accomplished man. He remarried after Aunty Charles's death and lived another 25 years, but Michigan never played a role in his second marriage. He wrote his memoirs in 1945. Aunty Charles and the Smith children are mentioned only once in passing. The summers in Michigan and the relationship with Ernest Hemingway (by then a prominent author) are not mentioned at all.[88] He is buried in Bunker Hill, Illinois.

The fourth Smith child, Merrill, was the oldest, born in 1883. But he, like Unk Charles, has faded from the Hemingway saga. He attended medical school at Washington University in St. Louis, but is not associated with the Hemingways. Merrill Smith died at Jewish Hospital in St. Louis of a burst appendix in 1924 at age 40.

Six months later Aunty Charles's youngest brother John died in September 1924, at age 56 from gastroenteritis that may have been linked to a very serious infection like typhoid. The month before, the

K. M. Durand Family/James Durand

Merrill Neville Smith *(1883-1924). He was the only one of the Smith family to have children—a daughter, Katherine Smith Durand (1919-2010). In fact, his parents were the only ones in their respective families to have any children as well.*

St. Louis Post-Dispatch ran an article about the number of typhoid deaths in the city, and another paper declared germ-spreading houseflies as being a "contaminating monster."[89]

He was the third in the family to die in 1924, starting with Aunty Charles. Her brother John is buried near her in the family plot at Riverview Cemetery. Nephew Merrill is not buried with his family in Louisiana, Mo., but rather in Fayette, Mo., his birthplace and hometown of his wife. He was a doctor there for his entire (albeit brief) career. Some biographers of the Hemingway circle overlook Merrill completely.

Hemingway's Big Break

The relationship between Ernest and the Smiths is a story covering the decade from 1916 to 1926. Though both the Smiths and the Hemingways had been going up to the same general area since the 1890s, the families never really had a chance to interact until they were both located at Horton Bay on the "isthmus" between the lakes — the Charles Farm being purchased in 1913 and Hemingway's Longfield Farm in 1905. These properties put the two families together with the Dilworth Inn on the common ground between them. Ernest helped chop wood and harvest apples from the orchard at Charles Farm, and Bill Smith would dig potatoes and pull beans from Dr. Hemingway's Longfield Farm.

"The Three Day Blow" takes place at Charles Farm. "Up in Michigan," another of the Hemingway stories, takes place in the town just east of Charles Farm, and "The End of Something" is set on the opposite side of the lagoon at "the point." The three locations form a triangle around the water feature called Horton Bay. The stories were published as a package. A fourth story "Summer People" was delayed by censorship (Nick Adams has sex with a woman named Katy) and is also is set on Charles Farm.[90] It wasn't published until 1972.

When Ernest returned from World War I as a wounded ambulance driver, Michigan became the starting point for his new life. Much of his recuperation from his wounds took place in the Michigan countryside (which would inspire many of his later short stories). He made connections there that led to newspaper jobs in

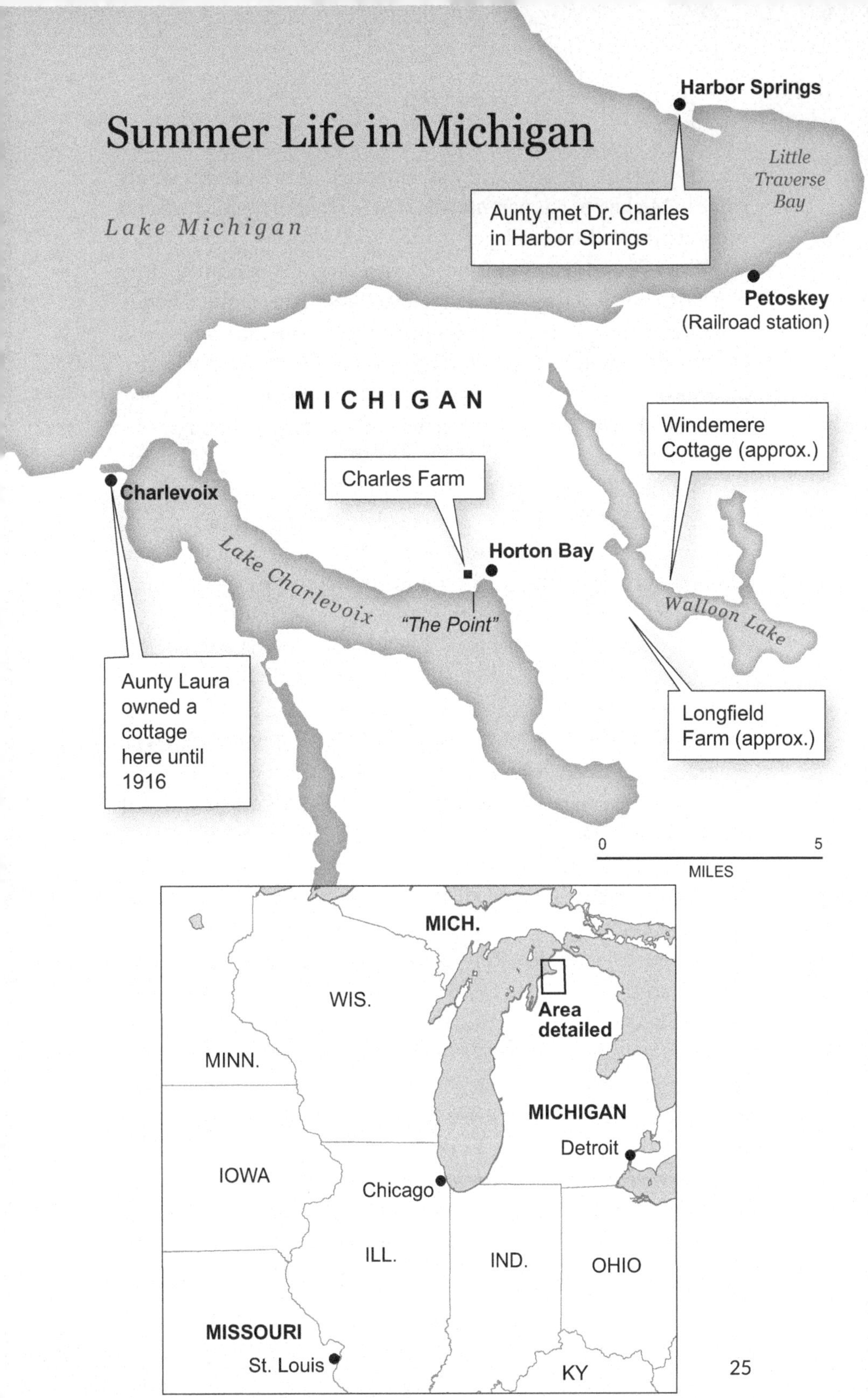

Summer Life in Michigan
Lake Michigan
Harbor Springs
Little Traverse Bay
Aunty met Dr. Charles in Harbor Springs
Petoskey
(Railroad station)
MICHIGAN
Windemere Cottage (approx.)
Charles Farm
Charlevoix
Horton Bay
Lake Charlevoix
"The Point"
Walloon Lake
Aunty Laura owned a cottage here until 1916
Longfield Farm (approx.)
0
5
MILES
MICH.
WIS.
Area detailed
MINN.
MICHIGAN
Detroit
IOWA
Chicago
ILL.
IND.
OHIO
MISSOURI
St. Louis
KY

Kansas City and Toronto, but was supported entirely by his family while in Michigan. His parents were not in favor of his idleness and wanted him to attend college.

When he returned to Chicago, in 1920, it was clear that he needed to find a place to live. He connected with his military buddy Bill Horne, who would be his roommate. Hearing that Ernest was looking to live in Chicago, Bill Smith put Ernest in touch with his brother Y.K. He was an established advertising man and was impressed by the young man who had befriended his siblings.

Doodles was away studying music in New York, so Y.K.'s apartment on East Division had plenty of room. And Y.K. was more than happy to make room for another creative soul in their place. Plus, a big one for Hemingway, was the fact that Katy was living there already, rooming with her friend Edith Foley.[91] Ernest and Bill Horne moved in at the end of the summer season in 1920.

Y.K. and his sister Katy lived and breathed the arts from Y.K.'s "domicile."[92] Y.K. began introducing Ernest to other artists and writers in the neighborhood. And, finally, Ernest found a job.

He started working for *The Cooperative Commonwealth*, a slick magazine run by a slick businessman.[93] His world was starting to come together, but he longed to go back to Italy where he had served during the war. One of Y.K.'s literary friends, the author Sherwood Anderson, gave Ernest alternate advice—you don't want to be in Italy; Paris is where it's at![94] All the St. Louis ducks were in a row on East Division Street. It was time for Hemingway's big break.

As autumn unfolded, Katy decided to invite a family friend and Mary Institute classmate to Chicago. Her friend needed a boost. She had been isolated and depressed caring for her sick mother, who had just passed away. So, here came Hadley Richardson through Hemingway's door. She arrived in October and stayed three weeks.[95] Hadley was struck by the bachelor traffic that moved through Y.K.'s apartment.

She was especially taken with one of the new tenants in the apartment—the young Ernest Hemingway. She liked his red cheeks and brown eyes as he straddled the piano bench; he liked her red

Theising photo

Grave marker for ***Laura Merrill "Aunty" Charles****, at the Riverview Cemetery in Louisiana, Mo. A modest marker for a gigantic personality.*

hair, the length of her skirt, and her talent at the piano.[96] A double date ensued. Ernest and Hadley went out with Bill Horne and Katy, enjoying dinner and cigarettes. The courtship was on. A marriage loomed for 1921. Paris beckoned.

Charles Farm was vacant after Aunty Charles died in 1924 and had become dilapidated. Bill became sick with tuberculosis about that time and had to spend months in a sanatorium.[97] Bill and Katy, who inherited Charles Farm, made a trip back to Horton Bay in 1929 and were shocked to find the house "stripped and gutted by local boys and neighbors."[98] Bill longed for the old times in Horton Bay but remarked to a friend how boring it had all become; there was no trace of what had been and it made him want to be back on Cape Cod. They repaired the place enough to sell it and used the money to purchase the Arequipa house in Provincetown, a house that would be the last home to the "Smooley Hall" crowd—and Dos Passos would become part of them when he married Katy later that year.[99]

After the death of Aunty Charles, Bill Smith rekindled his relationship with Ernest that had been strained in 1922, joining him in Pamplona for the 1925 bullfight season. Ernest and Hadley would have their own troubles in 1924, with St. Louisans being both the cause and the solution.

But that was around the corner. The first chapter is over. The Smiths had changed Ernest's life forever. Bill Smith connected Ernest with a fertile place to live, Katy Smith introduced him to the woman who would become his wife, and Y.K. Smith hosted it all. Things were moving fast for the young Hemingway, with more people from St. Louis heading into his life.

One last visit before heading off to World War I. From left: ***Madelaine "Sunny" Hemingway, Carl Edgar, Bill Smith, Charles Hopkins, Grace Hall Hemingway, Ernest*** *affectionately looking at his mother,* ***Marcelline Hemingway*** *(kneeling), and* ***Ursula Hemingway*** *(who would commit suicide in 1966).*

Ernest Hemingway Foundation of Oak Park, through Illinois Digital Archives MHS34

John F. Kennedy Library, EHPH05010

***Ernest** courting **Hadley** in St. Louis, in the back yard at Cates Avenue, May 1921. Hadley loved how Ernest would blow smoke from his nose, according to the Baker biography (1969, p. 79).*

2

The Richardson Family

"Allah be praised that we are living in the same time and know each other."[1]

Hadley in 1921 after a double-date with
Katy Smith and Bill Horne

The First Mrs. Hemingway

If we owe Hemingway's introduction to Hadley and being steered toward life in 1920s Paris to the brothers and sister Smith, then we owe his success in Paris to Hadley Richardson. The trust fund enabled by the Richardson Drug Company gave Ernest time and resources to build his career.

There are several biographies of Elizabeth Hadley Richardson and this work is not intended to duplicate them. The Sokoloff 1973 biography was written during Hadley's lifetime and Hadley played a part in its writing. Diliberto's 1992 work is impressive. She had the cooperation of the Usher family (descendants of Hadley's sister Fonnie). The book included family photos, especially of the old houses that are long gone.

Hadley was born in St. Louis on Nov. 9, 1891, the youngest of four surviving children of James and Florence Richardson. There

---

About the photo at left: *Some have said this was from Ernest's March visit instead of his May visit. There are too many leaves on the trees for this to be a March winter scene in St. Louis—though Ernest is described in his March visit as wearing similar clothes, likely the same suit for both visits. The weather in St. Louis on March 11-13 was unseasonably warm (60's) but the branches would still have been bare.*

were two lost pregnancies in the middle, so there was a large gap between the oldest two children, James Jr. ("Jamie") born in 1879 and Dorothea in 1880 and the younger two, Florence ("Fonnie") in 1889 and Hadley. The family lived in a luxurious home on Cabanne Avenue, one of the wealthy streets of St. Louis's near north side.

A Courtship in St. Louis

During Hadley's three-week stay in Chicago in 1920, the courtship began. Ernest was attracted to Hadley and Hadley was attracted to Ernest. She saw him as a pathway out of the confines she felt for the first decade of her adulthood. Hadley's predicament at age 29 cannot be understated. She was sad, depressed, and forlorn. On the verge of spinsterhood, she was getting ready for the potentially lonely life looming ahead. She watched her friend Katy Smith pulling away on a different, more exciting path. So, when Ernest Hemingway offered her a chance out, she embraced it thoughtfully and intentionally.

Both her parents were gone by the time she entered this new phase of life, but she was not without close family. She was not alone. Aunty Charles and The Doctor "were like second parents to me," she said, and she believed that Ernest loved them (though the historical record would indicate otherwise).[2]

On Valentine's Day of 1921, Ernest sent Hadley a telegram, warning her not to believe anything Aunty Charles said about him. He said he hated Aunty and The Doctor, according to biographer Peter Griffin. Hadley said to Ernest in her mind he was "untouched by anything, no matter what you do that may meet with the disapproval of Mrs. Charles." She added, "We are simpatico—fit in every way."[3]

Ernest made two trips to St. Louis during a courtship that went on for about 10 months, though he was invited for more. Hadley wanted him to attend a New Year's party at the posh University Club thrown by her friends, the Breakers. Ernest said he did not have the money for a train ticket, which hurt Hadley's feelings. She retaliated by attending the party with another man then telling Ernest all about it.[4]

Ernest's first visit was on March 11, 1921, arriving at St. Louis Union Station, perhaps the most opulent railroad station in the United States. Within two decades of that date, one-third of the United States' population was traveling through St. Louis Union Station going in one direction or another.

Hadley met him at the station and described him vividly. He wore a new Brooks Brothers three-piece suit, carried his Italian officer's cape he kept from his wartime adventure, and a valise that he picked up in Milan.[5] He was looking quite dapper.

Hadley picked him up with her friend Helen Breaker in Helen's electric car.[6] They drove from Union Station to Hadley's home at 5739 Cates Avenue (the second floor), an over-under duplex she shared with her sister Fonnie Usher and brother-in-law Dr. Roland Usher, which had the address 5737 Cates (the ground floor).[7] The two addresses shared the same entry door and the staircase to the upstairs was open. Ernest stayed with Aunty Charles at her recently purchased home on luxurious Westminster Place.[8]

Hemingway visited Hadley at her apartment four days and three nights, with each visit ending past midnight—something that must not have sat well with Aunty Charles. The evenings were still chaperoned, though, with sister Fonnie on the first floor flat and Hadley's friends, Ruth Bradfield and Bertha Doane, staying over in the extra rooms of her own upstairs flat.[9] They were not alone in any significant meaning of the word.

They enhanced their mutual attraction during the short visit and by spring, they were discussing marriage. Hadley still had other suitors, but none compared in her eyes to Ernest.

On April 11, 1921, Hadley joined her friends George and Helen Breaker, Ruth Bradfield, and "Doc" Lee Gay for a day of relaxation at the Meramec Highlands resort. (Doc and Ruth would eventually marry.)[10] They enjoyed hikes through the rolling hills, Prohibition cocktails, and some music and dancing. Though Hadley was physically present, her thoughts were elsewhere, dreaming of Ernest. She reported all of her dates to Ernest in letters.

Another doctor, Tony Day, picked up Hadley later that spring and they "zoomed out" in his fancy car to the Busch's Grove, where they had a "cute dinner" in "funny little screened-in houses" outdoors.[11] After that, they drove out Litzsinger Road looking for future picnic sites.[12] Hadley felt a little guilty after that date.

But Ernest made another trip to St. Louis on Memorial Day weekend, arriving May 27. He traveled with his friend and Chicago roommate Bill Horne and this time slept at Hadley's.[13] She had just recovered from a rather severe bout of pinkeye infection. She thought of Ernest while she was enduring Dr. Charles's treatments and poured out her soul in letters—reflecting on his eyes and their power over her, and his hands, and... she wrote abruptly "I'll stop analyzing."[14] Ernest's announcement of his Memorial Day visit perked her up! There are several well-published photographs of this visit, showing them sitting on a bench in Hadley's back yard.

The weekend was filled with fun. Bill Horne and Ruth Bradfield joined in and the foursome prepared big meals, made homemade wine from fermented raisins, played tennis in Forest Park, and picnicked there too.[15] The highlight of the weekend was a canoe trip on the Meramec River, stopping along the shores for a picnic and conversation.[16] Bill was smitten with Ruth, and to them the romance budding between Hadley and Ernest was clear. Indeed, it was. It was this weekend Ernest and Hadley formalized their engagement, deciding to keep the news secret for the time being.

Hadley's sister Fonnie, however, used the weekend to discourage them. She pulled Ernest aside and laid out Hadley's faults—before questioning him about his sexual history and any diseases he may have contracted.[17] Fonnie then shared her negative opinion with Aunty Charles, who was not excited about Ernest.

While in St. Louis on the canoe trip, Ernest drank too much and became obnoxious. He apologized in a letter afterward.[18] Hadley wasn't about to listen to Fonnie or Aunty Charles. Nor did she care about the drinking—she was in love. Ernest was furious with Fonnie.

Instead of giving-in to the family pressures, they decided to announce their engagement to the St. Louis circles and on June 14, 1921, George and Helen Breaker hosted an engagement party for Hadley and Ernest.[19] It was to be a surprise announcement for the guests, at a Tuesday afternoon tea in their sumptuous home at 5227

Westminster Place—on the elite blocks west of Aunty Charles.[20] Thirty guests were invited, but half of them didn't show up due to inclement weather and other business.

Ernest Hemingway was one of the no-shows. He had just left St. Louis two weeks earlier and he could not get away from his job at the magazine for a weekday event. They discussed in advance, though, what to say about their age difference (Hadley was to lie about Ernest's age) and stories to share about his war experience (so she could brag). His parents, however, sent a cable of congratulations that arrived at the party.[21] Hadley was happy her family dropped their resistance and gave her support (or at least curbed their active opposition).

The wedding was set for September in Michigan, and Hadley scheduled a month of vacation with George and Helen Breaker at a lake resort in Wisconsin leading up to it. She stopped on her way in Chicago to be with Ernest, arriving August 1. Ernest was still living with Y.K. Smith and so she stayed a week at the Virginia Hotel. She spent the days watching Ernest work at the magazine and they spent the rest of the time walking arm-in-arm through vibrant Chicago. Hadley was amazed by the bustling life that was unfolding in front of her—starkly different from her oppressive reality in St. Louis.

This was when they made love for the first time, taking turns in the passive partner role. Scholars who look closely at sexual themes in Hemingway's work make note of his want to transcend individual sexual roles.[22]

For example, consider the haircut discussions in *Garden of Eden, The Sun Also Rises,* and *Farewell to Arms*—all have examples of women characters having their hair cut in boyish styles to appear more like the men.[23] Also, three of his four wives had haircuts almost the same. Hadley's hair was cut in a short bob (she had it cut on their wedding day!), and Pauline's hair looked almost exactly like Ernest's at the time of their marriage. Fourth wife Mary also had the close-cropped haircut that he admired.

After her Chicago visit, Hadley was utterly lovestruck. Before she left to meet the Breakers in Wisconsin, she realized she had left her umbrella at Y.K.'s apartment, left her jewelry in the hotel safe, and left Ruth Bradfield's bridesmaid hat on the train—all of which took her quite a bit of time to retrieve.[24] By the time she arrived in Wisconsin, she was sick with a severe strep throat and the weather was not good either for her health or for recreation.[25]

Parental Dysfunction: "I didn't feel a desperate loss..."

Both of Hadley's parents had died by the year she was married, but the memory of her mother and father and their illustrious family members were never far from their youngest daughter as she prepared for the big day.

Hadley's mother, Florence Wyman, was born into one of St. Louis' wealthy families. Florence was the 8th of 9 children of Edward Wyman and Elizabeth Hadley, who died at 39 giving birth to child #9 when Florence was 3 years old. Florence's father was a professor who started the Wyman Institute in Alton, Ill., later called the Western Military Academy.[26] He later remarried and lived in Westminster Place, blocks away from where Aunty Charles lived in 1920.

Florence had five highly successful brothers who survived to adulthood: Dr. Walter Wyman, who was the third Surgeon General of the United States, serving from 1891 to 1911, during which time he was instrumental establishing tuberculosis sanatoriums; Frank Wyman, who lived at 5845 Cabanne Ave. and was appointed Postmaster of St. Louis by Theodore Roosevelt; Henry Wyman, who was Assistant Postmaster under Frank; Arthur Wyman, who moved to Chicago and was assistant to the president of the Chicago Railway Equipment Company; and Charles Wyman, who lived at 5523 Cabanne Ave. before moving to the suburb of Webster Groves and was a wholesaler and importer, as well as a U.S. Customs official for a time.

Florence married James Richardson in 1878, and they soon bought a grand home at 5632 Cabanne Ave. between the houses of her brothers Frank and Charles. James' father was also James Richardson, the founder of the prosperous Richardson Drug Co., a firm that grew into the largest pharmaceutical house west of the Mississippi with an inventory worth $14 million in today's dollars.[27]

Theising Collection

Detail of a billing statement from the ***Richardson Drug Company's*** *office in Omaha, 1890. Young James Richardson drove the St. Louis branch to ruin, yet the company continued to succeed from its Omaha branch.*

James' brother was Clifford, who became a partner in the family business by age 23.

The younger James Richardson, Florence's husband and Hadley's father, lived off the wealth of the family drug company. He "seemed to lack all ambition," was a disappointment to his father, held only a symbolic job at the family firm, and was prone to brooding, gambling, and drinking.[28]

He met Florence at the First Presbyterian Church on fashionable Lucas Place in St. Louis, where she was the organist. Biographer Diliberto's summation of their unlikely courtship was blunt: she did not have many suitors and he was a man who could be dominated. Her domination led to his alcoholism, said granddaughter Dodie Usher.[29]

Florence was a petulant woman. She was dedicated to feminism and women's suffrage, but despite giving birth to six children, she believed the births after the third child as "minor works" of "oversexed" parents.[30] Hadley was surviving child number four.

Florence loathed sex and wrote an essay for the *New Republic* in June 1915 [31] where she said intercourse should be "occasional and rare," that frequent sex is "abuse" and a waste of bodily fluid that could fuel other noble causes and urged women to revolt against the sexual desires of their husbands.[32] Daughter Fonnie (Hadley's sister) recalled that over the staircase of their sprawling mansion hung a copy of Saraceni's *Judith Holding the Head of the General Holofernes* in a bloody depiction of a biblical story, where the lovely Judith seduces then decapitates the drunken general who threatened the Israelites.[33] Florence was altogether a cold spouse and a distant mother at home.

She did, however, play a dynamic role in her community, especially in the St. Louis suffrage movement. Her life can best be described as "plain living and high thinking" according to a 1914 feature about her.[34] In reality, "the household suffered from [an] overwrought sense of duty and respectability" that James was quick to violate.[35]

Hadley found some escape from her oppressive mother through her best childhood friend, Elsa Blackman, whose sister married the author Orrick Johns.[36] With Elsa, Hadley could pour out her soul. Through Elsa's family, she was introduced to the appeal of intellectual discussion circles with St. Louis's literary elite that included such writers as Kate Chopin, William Marion Reedy, Zoe Atkins, Sara Teasdale, and many others.[37] She rode the streetcar to Webster Groves to spend time with her English teacher, who showered the young woman with access to the literary classics.[38] Mother Florence had these circles too, but Hadley was not part of them. Though Hadley did not learn many of the lessons of life that a popular young woman would, she had enough friends to show her that another side existed.

Hadley's father James did not share Florence's artistic and community appreciation, and rebelled against his bitter wife. He drove the St. Louis office of the Richardson Drug Co. into the ground, leaving only the Omaha headquarters.[39] He took a face-saving "consulting" vice presidency with the J. H. McLean Medicine Company—a highly-successful quack-medicine house in St.

FINANCIAL WORRY CAUSE OF SUICIDE

JAMES RICHARDSON DEAD

Member of Prominent Family Kills Himself in Cabanne Home.

Newspapers.com; public domain

Headline announcing the death of ***James Richardson,*** *1905 in the St. Louis Globe-Democrat. The description of the death scene was graphic. Hadley remarked that they were not close and she did not feel a great sense of loss.*

Louis—but he was generally a failure at business. After his father's death in 1893, James and his brother Clifford inherited annual proceeds from the thriving Richardson Drug Co. in Omaha amounting to $30,000 annually ($850,000 today). Clifford used his annual investment proceeds to found the Chemical National Bank of St. Louis and help construct the Chemical Building at the corner of Eighth and Olive. (The Richardson Memorial Library at the St. Louis Art Museum is named for him.) James lost all of his wealth gambling in the stock market and on quack medicine investments.

On Feb. 8, 1905, Hadley's father, James Richardson, shot himself. The coverage of the death in the *St. Louis Globe-Democrat* was graphic. He was found in a pool of blood in his "luxuriously furnished bedroom" still clutching a revolver. "Appearances indicated that he had arisen from bed, stood before the large mirror of his dressing room in his night clothes, and deliberately placed the weapon behind his right ear before pulling the trigger."[40]

Hadley said she was sad but "I didn't feel a desperate loss" because "I was never terribly close to him."[41] The suicide triggered a liquidation of the estate, including the family home, to pay his debts. The other members of the Richardson clan responded, though, with trusts that would ensure a level of comfort for the surviving relatives.

There were also life insurance settlements amounting to nearly $20,000 (about $560,000 in today's dollars). The Richardsons also bought a house on Cates Avenue, just one block west and one block south of their old home. In terms of social prestige, it might well have been 100 miles. The house was on a narrow lot behind the modest Episcopal Church of the Ascension.

This was the house where Hadley and Fonnie were living on different floors when Hemingway paid his first courting visit to St. Louis. The duplex had two addresses. Diliberto describes it as a three-story frame house to which mother Florence had a brick addition built at the rear that was "ugly but comfortable" according to Hadley.[42] Based on maps of the neighborhood near the time of purchase, the initial house started out as #5737 and the address #5739 likely was added when the addition was made.[43] It would not have been difficult to have a new street address made, since her mother's brother was the Postmaster at the time.

National Archives and Records Administration; Theising Collection

Professor ***Roland G. Usher*** *(1880-1957) in his 1920 passport photo. Usher went to England that year for respite from his celibate marriage, presumably to have an affair. He contracted tuberculosis later and spent much of 1921 in a sanatorium on the East Coast. He missed Hadley and Ernest's wedding.*

Like Mother, Like Daughter—In All the Wrong Ways

Fonnie was a mirror of her mother. Mother Florence was a staid critical woman who did not care for fashion or alcohol, but admired the arts and politics. Fonnie was the favorite and Florence didn't mind if everyone knew it. She participated in social events, and one year was part of the queen's court at the Veiled Prophet ball—the highest of St. Louis social events.[44]

At an Artists' Guild event Florence met a young man with a Harvard degree and a professorship at Washington University in St. Louis: Roland Greene Usher. In 1909, she introduced Fonnie to Roland, a romance ensued, and they married in 1910.[45]

There was a double standard in the household when it came to Hadley and Fonnie. "My mother was crazy about Fonnie," said Hadley years later.[46]

Fonnie and Roland had four children. The first was yet another Florence (called "Fonchen") in 1911, followed by Roland Jr. in 1914, Dodie in 1918, and Richard in 1920. Hadley was not fond of the eldest, though from photographs she appears to have spent a considerable amount of time with her. She wrote to Ernest in 1921 that her niece was "a rather unpleasant little party—a she-devil at times." The little one managed to annoy the "sweet as peaches" Bill Horne on his Memorial Day visit with Hemingway.[47]

Fonnie was having her own emotional problems at the time of Hadley's courtship and engagement. Her marriage was a wreck early on and she showed signs of emotional instability.[48] After the birth of their fourth child in April 1920, she had stopped having sex with her husband. Roland asked his brother Abbot, a professor at Harvard, to speak with Fonnie about the importance of a good physical relationship between husband and wife.[49] But things didn't work out and Roland could not handle the strain. He left for Europe alone in the summer of 1920 and, presumably, had an affair. He was sent to a sanatorium at some point in Massachusetts, not returning until January 1922.[50]

Fonnie publicly claimed to like Ernest but in truth instantly disliked and distrusted him.[51] Fonnie was out of sorts over her sister's pending marriage. When she had taken Ernest aside during his trip and tried to dissuade him from marrying Hadley, she told him Hadley was selfish, lazy, and frail.[52] These were the same criticisms Hadley's mother had made about her over the years. Hemingway vehemently disagreed.

Fonnie was also out of sorts over her finances. With Roland in the sanatorium in Massachusetts, he was not earning any money as a professor. She began renting extra rooms of the duplex where Hadley and her mother had lived prior to Mother Florence's death. Hadley's friends were there at the time of Ernest's Memorial Day visit. Bill Smith reported this as his address in the 1920-21 St. Louis city directory.[53] There may have been other boarders.[54]

The angered Ernest Hemingway did what he often did when upset: he wrote something vicious. Though unpublished, his poem with the shocking title "Passion for the [Negroes][55]" starts out criticizing Fonnie Richardson by name, then her tenants in abstract, whom Ernest suggests Fonnie cared about only for their rent. In the strict segregation of St. Louis in the day, African Americans would never have been tenants in the neighborhood, though to Fonnie's credit, she was an advocate for civil rights and invited African American leaders to dine in her home—which did not go unnoticed by neighbors and obviously Ernest. He ranted against little Fonchen in the poem and said he wished harm to her. Diliberto notes that Fonnie probably never saw the poem, but Hadley did and refused to discuss it years later with Hemingway biographer Carlos Baker, only saying, "It's too horrible!"[56]

Hadley, being eight years older than Ernest on the eve of their marriage, wondered about her fertility. She exploded when Fonnie, who had been taking some psychology classes at the University Club, took it upon herself to speak with Dr. Sidney Isaac Schwab, a prominent neurologist and psychiatrist who had treated Hadley years earlier.[57] The doctor said Hadley should not have children for six years due to her mental state and advised her not to get married at all.

Hadley also had thought of consulting the city's first gynecologist the year before, but concluded to herself she was in such "rotten shape" she didn't want to hear what he would have to say.[58] This doctor was Dr. George Gellhorn—the father of Martha Gellhorn, the woman who would be Hemingway's third wife.

Mother Florence belittled Hadley over the years and Hadley turned that anger inward. Hadley cared for her mother full-time during Florence's declining years and had to endure her mother's daily admonishments. They argued constantly and hurled cruelty at each other. Florence must have been in a wheelchair. Though Ernest never met her, he referred to her as the "bitch on wheels."[59]

After her mother's death, Hadley wanted out of her oppressive home environment for good. She confronted Fonnie over the meddling in her relationship with Ernest and told Fonnie to stop. When Ernest's parents offered to pay for the wedding at the church in Horton Bay, Hadley leaped at the offer to get the wedding out of St. Louis and away from Fonnie's grip.[60] Fonnie felt relief at not having to pay for the wedding during tight financial times and Hadley suggested she use the money to hire someone to take care of her children so she could come to the wedding. Fonnie may have bought the new dress, but her daughter, Fonchen, was at the wedding anyway.

MRS. F. W. RICHARDSON, SUFFRAGE LEADER, DIES

Was Instrumental in Founding of Suffrage League, Piano Club and Symphony Society Here.

Newspapers.com; public domain

Obituary for ***Florence Richardson****, 1920 in the St. Louis Post-Dispatch. She was an activist in the community and oppressive at home. Her death was freeing for Hadley, who said her mother's words "lay like lumps of lead in my heart" (Griffin 183).*

Marrying Her Way out of St. Louis

Hadley arrived in Horton Bay for her wedding early on Friday, Sept. 2, 1921.[61] The wedding was set for the next day. She stayed at Charles Farm, conveniently located near the church and reception site. As soon as Hadley arrived, Aunty Charles shared her misgivings about Ernest one last time.

She said he had broken her niece Katy's heart, she felt. He was feuding with her nephew Y.K. He was self-centered and would be a difficult husband. Hadley wasn't moved, extolling Ernest's virtues from her perspective. Aunty Charles gave in: "Well, if he's like that, he's ideal."[62]

Hadley got her hair cut on the morning of her wedding by her artistic friend Helen Breaker. Ernest liked short hair on a woman so Hadley had Helen cut her hair back. After the job was done she washed her hair in the almost-frigid lake.[63]

Aunty Charles enjoyed planning parts of the wedding, but was surprisingly distant from Dr. and Mrs. Hemingway (who were paying for the wedding). At a dinner that evening, Ernest was the only member of the Hemingway household invited.[64] Hadley's bridal party was also headquartered at Charles Farm on Lake Charlevoix while Ernest and his group were based at the Dilworth cottages and Windemere.

The next day, both bride and groom spent time with friends on their respective lakes prior to the wedding, waiting for the scheduled 4 p.m. start. The Dilworth Inn was the place for final preparations and the celebration afterward.

At about 3 p.m., Hadley came in from washing her newly shortened thick hair. There was a brief panic in getting it to dry enough to put on her veil, but the problem was solved and the wedding started just fifteen minutes later than planned.[65] Plenty of photographs from the day survive; Hadley looks relaxed before and after the event.

Prior to the wedding there had been some consternation about who would escort the bride down the aisle. Hadley wanted her brother Jamie to do the honor as a stand-in for their late father, but he was being treated for tuberculosis at a sanatorium and couldn't

***Hadley** in her wedding attire, at the home of Aunty Charles in Horton Bay, Michigan. Aunty Charles actually booked a room for herself at the Petoskey Inn during this time according to a news report. Hadley's friend, Helen Pierce Breaker (1891-1936), may have taken this artful photo. She became a photographer of note in Europe in the last decade of her life.*

John F. Kennedy Library, EHPH05726

Ernest and his men

Wedding at Horton Bay, September 3, 1921

Many have struggled to identify all the men in this photo. I've examined the choices and compared their respective ages, physical descriptions from their passport and military records, and other extant photos, and feel that I've properly identified all of them. No one has recognized George Breaker before, and I'm confident that he is in the photo. The person who may have been there, or not, is high school friend John Lewis "Jack/Jock" Pentecost Jr. (1898-1955). Clarence's announcement said he was there, but we know his list had errors and that many Oak Park area families did not make the trip. Some have identified either Jenkins or Hopkins as Pentecost, but I've verified both with other photos. A request to the Pentecost family for a photo was unanswered as of this writing.

Photo courtesy of the Hemingway Foundation of Oak Park, through Illinois Digital Archives AEHF-MHS387

Howell Griffiths Jenkins
of Chicago, ambulance-driving friend (1894-1971)

George J. Breaker
of St. Louis, who escorted the bride (1891-unknown)

Charles Hains Hopkins
Ernest's editor friend at the Kansas City Star (1893-1956)

Charlie Hopkins moved to the St. Louis area in 1934 to do advertising for the Western Cartridge Co. and eventually became an executive with Olin Corp. in nearby East Alton, Ill. He was a noted conservationist and died at age 62. He is buried near his family's land in Oklahoma—acquired in 1903, Indian Territory days.

William Dodge Horne Jr.
of Yonkers but living in Chicago, usher at the wedding, roommate in Chicago, and ambulance-driving friend (1892-1985)

Luman Carleton Ramsdell
friend from Petoskey, Mich. who traveled with Dutch (1900-1928)

Ernest

Edwin "Dutch" Pailthorp
usher, friend from Petoskey (1900-1972)

William Benjamin Smith Jr.
of St. Louis, best man and a subject of this book (1895-1972)

Joseph Charles "Carl" Edgar
Michigan friend from Kansas City who traveled with Hopkins (1889-1956)

Carl Edgar was the son of Charles Bloomfield Edgar, a very successful businessman who was born in St. Louis and went through St. Louis public schools. Carl was named for his paternal grandfather, Joseph C. Edgar, a St. Louis architect who designed the Campbell House, now a museum in downtown St. Louis.

be at the wedding. Her brother-in-law Roland, Fonnie's husband, was her second choice but he, too, was institutionalized with TB and was unavailable. She then asked Dr. Joseph Charles, Aunty Charles's husband, to escort her. He was like a second father to her and was willing, but Ernest did not like Aunty and Unk and vetoed the choice. So Hadley finally settled on George Breaker, the lawyer and husband of her friend Helen Breaker. They were the hosts of the engagement party and Hadley had just spent the previous month with the couple in Wisconsin.[66]

With the cast present and accounted for, the Richardson-Hemingway wedding was simple and small. None of the Hemingway parents' friends in Oak Park accepted the invitation to travel to Michigan for the wedding, so Mrs. Hemingway invited the entire town of Horton Bay.

Hadley's radiant happiness was obvious as she walked up the aisle on the arm of George Breaker. Her bridal party included Fonnie as Matron of Honor and three attendants: George's wife Helen, Hadley's friend Ruth Bradfield, and Katy Smith, the woman who brought the bride and groom together, but who was slow to commit to attending the wedding and made it known she was not happy about it. Ernest was supported by best man Bill Smith, ushers Bill Horne and Dutch Pailthorpe, and friends from work and military service.[67]

"When Ernest and I were coming out of the church, he stepped on my white satin slipper," Hadley said to biographer Alice Sokoloff 50 years later. "I thought at the time that it was a bad omen, and I guess it was."[68] Hadley would not return to St. Louis in any substantive way ever again.

Trust-Fund Life in Paris

Ernest longed to return to Italy, where he served in World War I and first experienced the freedom of international travel. He referred to it pejoratively as "wopland" in his nickname-infused letters. He sold the idea of a trip to Hadley, but before he could arrange the journey he was introduced to the author Sherwood Anderson through Y.K. Smith. Anderson considered Paris as the place to be in post-war Europe and persuaded Ernest to join the band of writers who became "The Lost Generation" in Paris of the 1920s.

Think of it. Ernest Hemingway was then a writer of newspaper and magazine articles, paid a per-piece fee. He dreamed of a novel but only earned money from the peripheral edges of journalism. In order to make his life work as a fiction writer, he needed someone else to pay the bills.

And here was the source of the "filthy lucre" walking up the aisle and out of the church on his arm--Hadley Richardson Hemingway.[69] She was born into wealth she had nothing to do with. In fact, had her father been more responsible, she could have been fabulously wealthy like those in her circle (Aunty Charles, the Wymans, grandfather Richardson).

But Hadley was by no means middle class. She had her trust fund. Despite her father's destructive behavior, the family was able to provide her a trust fund of $60,000 (about $900,000 in today's dollars) that generated about $3,000 (about $38,000 today) a year.[70] That's pretty good income for simply standing still.

This was the money that funded their life in Paris. By not having to get a paying job, Ernest could write, gain experiences that fueled the writing, and consult with the group of writers minds that surrounded him in Paris—Gertrude Stein, Ezra Pound, and Scott Fitzgerald. In contrast, Pound, at about this time, lamented that St. Louis poet T. S. Eliot worked a day job as a banker so he could pursue his art—and even arranged a fundraiser for the poet.[71]

All went well for the newlyweds. Their son, John Hadley Nicanor Hemingway, was born in 1923. That same year, Hemingway's literary work was published for the first time—*Three Stories and Ten Poems*—then came the collection "*in our time*" in 1924. Things were going as they dreamed.

While 1924 was a good year for Ernest's writing career, it was a different story for the other subjects of this book. We have already reviewed what happened to the Smiths. Something almost as tragic was about to happen to the Hemingways. St. Louisans were at the heart of it all.

Newspapers.com; public domain

***George J. Breaker** in the St. Louis Star, 1927. He ran away to escape prosecution for fraud and other crimes. He squandered a portion of Hadley's wealth in his bad investment schemes in 1924. His wife Helen divorced him in 1926 after he defrauded her widowed mother.*

George Breaker escorted Hadley up the aisle in September of 1921. George and wife Helen were among Hadley's longest and most loyal friends. When George, an attorney in the financial industry, said Hadley should be mindful of her trust investments and that he might be able to get her much higher earnings than she was experiencing, she took his advice.

Hadley signed over management of one-third of her funds from the Mercantile Trust Company to George Breaker in that fateful year. She assumed her old friend would deliver on his promises, much in the same as Aunty Charles's real estate holdings were managed so well by her brother Leonard. The first sign of trouble was when an expected deposit was missing in March 1924.

Ernest had instructed George to be conservative in his investments, and after the missing payment, telegraphed that he should deliver the bonds back to

Mercantile, or deposit $7,400 due to Hadley.[72] It never happened. To Hadley's shock and dismay, George embezzled her money for some bad investments made for his bank.

This meant Hadley lost a third of her wealth and her income was reduced by $760 annually (over $11,000 in today's dollars).[73] The couple wasn't exactly destitute but in today's dollars, her income fell from $38,000 to $27,000 a year at a time the couple's expenses were increasing after the birth of their son. George hadn't lost all her money, but put a sizable dent in the Hemingways' financial cushion. The result wasn't just monetary, it also put a crimp in the security and clear head Hemingway needed to proceed with his literary efforts.

With Friends Like These

George J. Breaker was a St. Louis attorney, who by the way lived at 5227 Westminster near Aunty Charles.[74] His wife was born Helen Pierce, and grew up in one of the most exclusive addresses in the city: #39 Kingsbury Place, with her parents Lucie and Lawrence Pierce.[75]

Like so many wealthy St. Louisans, Lawrence Pierce amassed a fortune through real estate. He built the Pierce Building in downtown St. Louis, which for decades was the center of the insurance industry in the city. In the 1980s, the building became the Adams Mark Hotel, adjacent to the Gateway Arch grounds. The hotel has changed names today, but remains a prime piece of St. Louis real estate. After Lawrence's death, Lucie lived at their later luxurious address: #16 Hortense Place.[76]

George was invested heavily in the Allenton Bank.[77] Allenton was a small community on the far western edge of the St. Louis area—beyond the established suburbs of St. Louis, out by the Meramec River resorts Hadley and friends enjoyed for Sunday outings.

George hoped the nearby resorts would draw wealthy St. Louis families moving and investing west of the city for homes or vacation property. Places like Charlevoix and Horton Bay in Michigan saw these types of "vacation investments" hundreds of miles from

Chicago and far more distant from St. Louis. Breaker imagined what opportunity lay in a vacation investment only an hour from the city limits. He saw a sure thing!

But the sure-thing returns from the Meramec were not happening so George started making other investments in get-rich-quick schemes. George sought to protect his risk by investing in nearby marble quarries. He convinced Helen's widowed mother to invest.[78] It didn't work out.

He tried to cover his losses by throwing good money after bad in hotels and subdivisions in Texas and Florida, and picked up investors in New York, Chicago, and downstate Missouri. But then the work stopped. Bonds stopped selling. Revenues were not coming in. Hadley's money was part of these investments.

Auditors began asking questions. Things got rough. His business partner, John L. Crain, was questioned in the murder of another bank's attorney, Clifford Hicks, whose money was entangled with

This St. Louis WOMAN is Gaining Fame in Paris with Her ARTISTIC PHOTOGRAPHY

Mrs. Helen Pierce Breaker's works were among seven of a thousand selected for reproduction in one of the foremost publications of France, and the high quality of her products has gained her membership in the French Photographic Society.

out of soft voices—a real pleasure to listen to, whether the tongue is French or English.

And it is quite as likely to be one as the other, since Mrs. Breaker speaks both.

Says she, by way of explanation: "I found myself spending whole afternoons with French people. And French was the language of the afternoon! Of course, I couldn't bore them continually with Anglo-French platitudes. So I set out to learn—and studied hard—or at least until my French teacher refused to have me any more, telling me she could teach me no more."

But I rather think Mrs. Breaker is one of those lucky linguists, with ability to acquire languages readily and easily. She even adds German, to make a third language—due to a year's residence in that country.

How did Helen Pierce Breaker, who belongs to an old and well-known St. Louis family of wealth, happen to take up photography, in the first place? And how long has she been working at it?

Newspapers.com; public domain

1930 St. Louis Globe-Democrat feature on ***Helen Pierce Breaker's*** *success as a photographer in Paris. She remained close to the Hemingways. She committed suicide in Paris in 1936.*

Allenton Bank's. George Breaker got a ticket to South America and never returned. Indictments were issued later but were dropped in 1931.[79]

Helen divorced George in absentia, in an uncontested court action that took less than 48 hours from start to finish. She remained close to the Hemingways and moved to Paris, establishing herself as a "modestly successful" professional photographer, as Frederick Voss described it.[80] Her work was exhibited in Paris in 1929 and published in *L'Illustration*.

Her high-quality portraits of Ernest now are part of the Hemingway Collection at the Kennedy Library. In recent decades, an art photo was exhibited at the Guggenheim and auctioned by Sotheby's. Her photographs of Ernest are sincere and poignant. She was never blamed for the loss of money. Ill and losing her sight, she took her own life in 1936, almost 10 years exactly after her divorce and just weeks after her mother's death in St. Louis. She left behind a 60-page suicide note that took eight months to write.[81]

An Unexpected Dividend and a Life Away from St. Louis

Hadley and Ernest could not believe George Breaker's embezzlement. There soon, however, was a "never mind" quality to the effect on Hadley's trust fund and Hemingway's psyche. For suddenly the financial ship was righted in the Paris apartment when they received an unexpected dividend from St. Louis.

Florence Richardson's brother, Frank Wyman, the Postmaster of St. Louis, died April 24, 1924, about the time the Breaker scandal was revealed.[82] Hadley was out of touch with her St. Louis family, so it was a great surprise and relief when she learned she received an $8,000 inheritance from Wyman's estate.[83] This money canceled out most of the $11,000 loss from George Breaker and largely made the Hemingway couple whole again. The crisis George created only lasted a few months but his gross mismanagement did prevent them from enjoying even greater security during Ernest's most productive years. Paris was a transformative place. Ernest gave Hadley an escape from her suffocation in St. Louis and Hadley lifted Ernest to his great potential.

She had said of their marriage, "The world's a jail and we're going to break it together."[84]

***Ernest** and **Hadley's** passport photos for their 1923 renewals after the birth of their son. They were on the verge of a new world.*

National Archives and Records Administration; Theising Collection.

Hadley had been miserable in St. Louis. She took a man who was a writer among many writers, in a city (Chicago) that had many writers, and put him in a place where he could surpass those who went before him.

Ernest left Hadley in 1926 and finalized their divorce Jan. 27, 1927, shortly after *The Sun Also Rises* was released. He felt terribly guilty over the breakup and dedicated the manuscript to her. More significantly, he gave her the royalties from the book forever. (It has never been out of print.) When rage or insult filled him, he spewed it out in words and burdened others with its weight while enjoying the lift it gave to him. He often used people and rejected them before they could reject him, an immaturity that dogged his life and tainted his reputation.

In *A Moveable Feast*, his last book, he described Hadley as a heroine who was the only one in the Paris story who had a life that turned out well. Sure, he calls it fiction, but that's a protection for his failing memory more than a literary reality. Carlos Baker says Ernest phoned Hadley late in his life to help recall details of Paris—undoubtedly for *Feast*.[85] Hadley said in an interview late in her life, "I think Ernest was always fond of me, and I was always fond of him, but in the end I was glad to be out of those stormy seas." She added, "I had such a wonderful husband afterwards. That brought happiness again."[86]

A later edition of *Feast* (Simon and Schuster 2009) contains several of the false starts he wrote for the book. In the last of his false starts, everyone from Paris remembers something from their own lived perspective and what they got in return. And overall, *A Moveable Feast* is Hemingway's acknowledgment of the return he got from the Paris that Hadley—and she alone—provided him. Perhaps at the end, he was a mature man after all.

John F. Kennedy Library EHPH06940

***Ernest** and **Pauline** shortly after their marriage in 1927. Pauline adopted the boyish haircut that Ernest liked.*

3

The Pfeiffer Family

"All great men have been great workers, but not all great workers are great men."

Uncle Gus, April 1, 1937[1]

Fashion, Family, and a Rich Uncle

In March 1925, Pauline Pfeiffer and her sister Jinny (Virginia) were in Paris. Through mutual friends, the sisters knew Hadley and enjoyed her company. The Hemingways traveled in clusters and everything was a group activity. The sisters Pfeiffer also enjoyed being on the edge of these social circles that included American expatriate writers like Scott Fitzgerald and Ezra Pound. Pauline landed a job with *Vogue,* the prestigious U.S. fashion magazine and was said to be looking for a husband. At various times, Pauline expressed interest in Bill and Y.K. Smith, Harold Loeb, and Robert Benchley, another American writer.[2]

At Christmas time, Pauline joined Ernest and Hadley on a trip to Austria. While there, Pauline turned her attention away from Hadley toward Ernest. Pauline stayed with the Hemingways and sometimes climbed in bed with the couple for breakfast together.[3] Hadley noticed the increased attraction between the two, told herself it was nothing serious—a big mistake on Hadley's part for only a few months later, Ernest and Pauline were having an intimate affair. Ernest was wracked with guilt, and Pauline—who took her Catholic faith seriously—was too.[4]

But nothing stopped them and Hadley soon knew her marriage was doomed.

That summer of 1926, Hadley demanded that Ernest and Pauline separate for 100 days, a plan aimed at making sure everyone could get in touch with their true feelings, a plan that failed. She granted Ernest a divorce that was finalized in January 1927.

Hemingway finished his first novel, *The Sun Also Rises*, in August during the separation. He dedicated the book to Hadley and their son and gave future royalties to her. It was, he thought, the least he could do.[5] She enjoyed the payment from book sales and the subsequent movie rights for decades.

A year after the divorce, Hadley met Paul Scott Mowrer, a journalist and writer. After a five-year courtship they married in 1933, living the rest of their lives together, happily out of the public eye.

Ernest and Pauline married May 10, 1927, in Paris.

A new chapter of Ernest's life opened. In order to marry Pauline he agreed to convert to Catholicism. According to biographer Carlos Baker, he likely lied to the priest in Paris that he was baptized among the wounded soldiers in Italy during World War I.[6] In his introduction to a later edition of *A Moveable Feast,* Patrick Hemingway said his father converted through instruction and coursework, during which he learned the concept of "moveable feasts," holy days that changed dates from year to year based on the timing of Easter (e.g., Ash Wednesday).[7] Ernest said his conversion was a matter of his own sexual impotence and that prayer in the church of St. Joseph des Carmes in Paris restored his virility and paved the way to his conversion.[8]

Hemingway also decided following the marriage to leave Europe and return to the States. He began exploring the world—the Caribbean, Africa, and Cuba. He was becoming a successful author, but without the *Sun* royalties, he still worried about money. Enter his second St. Louis wife. Pauline (like Hadley) had a trust fund that provided monthly payments to support their lifestyle as well as generous Pfeiffer relatives to cover everything else.

By the time Hemingway married Pauline he was a different man than the one who had married Hadley. Pauline knew his ways. She promised to not stand in the way of his lifestyle, an approach that was fine for her when she was the focus of his attention but less so when she had to fight for it.

Pauline was also a writer—trained at the University of Missouri Columbia's School of Journalism—but she gave up her career to support her husband as his skill and his fame grew. She loved him dearly. She also gave up mothering their children to be with him, leaving them with nurse Ada Stern and later admitting to her son Gregory she had no patience for raising children. She nearly gave up her own life in a difficult childbirth to please Ernest. He used this childbirth experience as the model for the death of Catherine in the conclusion of *Farewell to Arms*.[9]

The Pfeiffer Empire in and out of St. Louis

Henry, Paul, and Gustavus Pfeiffer were three brothers (in a family of 10 children) who grew up in Iowa farm country steeped in the ways of hard work, kind spirit, and loving generosity. Each of the brothers became wealthy in their own way and their business relationships kept their families closely bonded throughout their lives.[10]

An allergy to flour opened the road to the Pfeiffer fortunes. Henry, the eldest, tried his hand at flour milling but was too sensitive for the work. Instead, he was hired as an apprentice in a pharmacy and at 23 years old passed the state regulatory exam.[11] His employer sold him the store and he thus became the first Pfeiffer engaged in the chemical business.

He was a sharp, aggressive young man and his business grew quickly. Instead of buying his candy for his drug store in five-pound boxes, he bought barrels of it wholesale and became the

Hemingway-Pfeiffer Museum and Educational Center [signature: Theising Collection]

Uncle Gus Pfeiffer. *He moved to St. Louis in 1901, living on Morgan Street (now Delmar Boulevard). He bankrolled large parts of Ernest's life in Key West.*

primary source for candy in Cedar Falls, Iowa. Instead of placing a small ad in the local paper, he bought a full page. When his landlord raised his rent, Henry bought adjacent lots and built his own store bigger and better than before.[12] In 1891, he sold his Iowa operations and moved to the big city, St. Louis, and got into the chemical business.

His first partner was John Egbert Allan, creating the Allan-Pfeiffer Manufacturing Co. that eventually located at 815-817 N. 7th St., the downtown site of today's America's Center convention complex.[13] The company struggled in the competitive chemical market of St. Louis where the Richardson Drug Co. and other prominent firms like Mallinckrodt already dominated, and another chemical giant, Monsanto, was about to be launched.

The fledgling Allan-Pfeiffer company faced a severe setback in 1895, just four years after its founding when a fire broke out that burned their laboratory as well as the paint, tobacco, and tallow companies in the adjacent buildings. The total damage was nearly $90,000 (about $2.75 million today).[14]

The business recovered, but in 1901 Pfeiffer and Allan parted ways with Allan keeping the name. The Allan-Pfeiffer Chemical Co. was a prominent firm in St. Louis for the next 20 years.

Theising Collection

Letterhead from the ***Allan-Pfeiffer Manufacturing Company****, 1892.*

Henry started over. He established the Pfeiffer Chemical Company in 1901 and invited his younger brothers, Paul and Gus, to join him in St. Louis. They operated out of facilities on North Commercial Street in today's Laclede's Landing district.[15]

The Pfeiffer brothers moved their families to town and lived on what is today Delmar Boulevard—Henry and Annie at #5515, Gus and Louise lived at #4602 (and later at 5101 Kensington—not far from the "Boy Next Door" address of 5135 made famous in the film *Meet Me in St. Louis*), and Paul and Mary at #5129, along with sons Karl and Max and their daughters Virginia and Pauline, the future Mrs. Hemingway.[16]

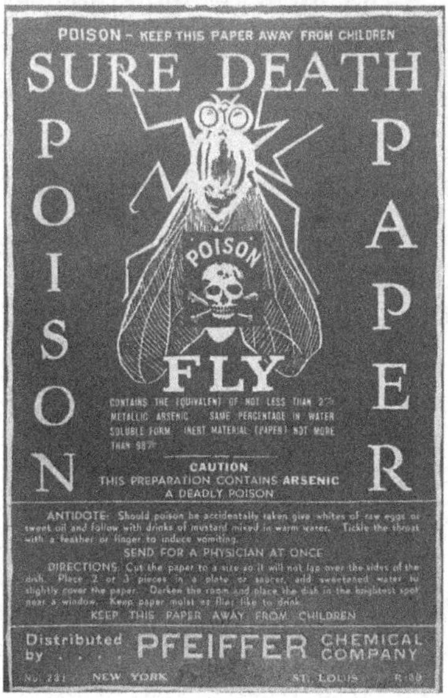

Theising Collection

***The Pfeiffer Chemical Company of St. Louis** sold household products like this fly paper, however it expanded more into medicines with the purchase of the Warner Company and later more into perfumes/cosmetics with the purchase of the Hudnut Company.*

Paul didn't take long to decide the chemical business was not for him and sold his share of the business to his brothers in 1902 and began to invest in land. Unlike his brothers, Paul retained part of the farm in Iowa and he started eyeing acreage in Arkansas. From his desk in the Pfeiffer Chemical offices, he started buying and selling land. Paul eventually controlled 63,000 acres of farmland in the cotton belt of Arkansas; some acquired for a dollar an acre.[17] He wanted to leave St. Louis and move to Arkansas but his wife Mary, a devout Catholic, was opposed. She was attached to the big city, its libraries and museums, its shopping and entertainment, and its flourishing Catholic institutions.

The Pfeiffer brothers arrived in the Mound City during its most exciting era, those years before, during, and immediately after the World's Fair and Olympic Games of 1904. But things began to change in 1908.

Paul's widowed mother died in 1908 and Mary's died in 1909. The Pfeiffer Chemical Co. of St. Louis bought a controlling interest in the William R. Warner Pharmaceutical Company in 1908,[18] and Henry and wife Anne moved away to Philadelphia where the growing empire was headquartered. Gus and Louise soon followed. In 1916 the firm bought up the Richard Hudnut Perfumery Co. and the whole operation moved to New York City, where Henry and Gus lived the rest of their lives.

Paul's wife, Mary, grew lonely in St. Louis. The parents were gone, Paul's siblings had moved, and Pauline, their oldest daughter, graduated from Visitation Academy on May 21, 1913. Paul still wanted to live near his cotton empire in Arkansas and Mary finally relented. The last of the St. Louis Pfeiffers moved to Piggott, Ark., where they bought a home at 1021 W. Cherry St. on July 4.

Today, this building is the Hemingway-Pfeiffer Museum and Educational Center, part of Arkansas State University. Pauline enrolled at the University of Missouri in Columbia and began her study of journalism (Katy Smith was enrolled there already). The Pfeiffer years in St. Louis were over.

Pauline went to work for the publishing house of the *Cleveland Press* after graduation from college in 1918. She lost the job soon after when she overstayed her leave for her brother's funeral that November, but wasn't unemployed for long. Her Uncle Gus, now in New York, knew Conde Nast, the publisher of *Vanity Fair* and *Vogue*. Pauline made an impression on Nast, whose mother was from St. Louis.[19] She started at *Vanity Fair* and soon transferred to *Vogue*—her ticket to Paris and into the arms of Ernest Hemingway.

Becoming Mrs. Hemingway

When Pauline returned home for the 100-day separation from Ernest, Uncle Gus met her at the dock in New York. He arranged

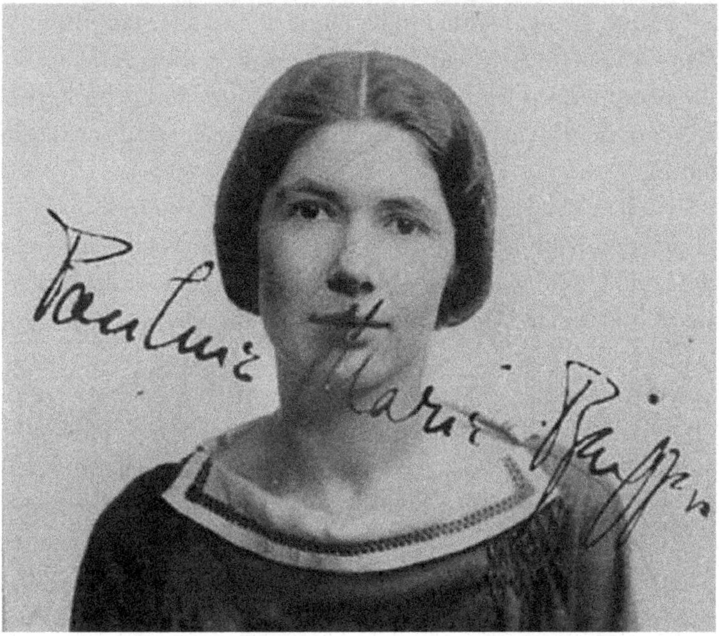

National Archives and Records Administration; Theising Collection

***Pauline's** signed passport photo from 1922, just before her first trip to Europe. She traveled with her friend Clara Dunn, visited Germany and Italy, and did newspaper work along the way according to the Hawkins biography.*

a room for her at the Waldorf-Astoria, but the room wasn't ready on time because the St. Louis Cardinals had defeated the Yankees in the 1926 World Series the night before and Cardinals fans were slow to leave in the morning. She wondered how she would tell her parents the news. Her mother, upon hearing, was brought to tears, not for Pauline, but rather at the thought of Hadley being abandoned. "How does *she* feel?" her mother kept asking.[21]

By then, Ernest was well known, both for his storytelling and his raucous, adventurous lifestyle. Paul and Mary Pfeiffer saw Ernest as a carousing drunkard who happened to find success through writing. They opposed the marriage. But Uncle Gus interceded and promptly telegraphed them after meeting Ernest, "Pauline could not marry a better or finer citizen than young Hemingway."[22]

Pauline deeply wanted to be married and she was willing to do what she had to do to accommodate Ernest. Biographer Carlos Baker summarized her position: "If Ernest would only hurry back to her, he could have his own way all the time, she would cross him in nothing."[23]

Ernest delayed telling his parents. They heard rumors, however, and pleaded with Ernest for the truth. Ernest wrote to his sister Madelaine ("Sunny"), swearing her to secrecy and explaining his divorce and remarriage to Pauline. He said his parents "have never merited my confidence nor backed me—and fond of them as I am I can't carry the extra weight of home criticism."[24]

On their wedding day in Paris, Pauline's mother wrote a letter from Piggott. She said she and Paul were sorry they could not be in Paris, and said they were praying for her. Then she spoke to Ernest in her letter, in a line that seems to echo the words of Aunty Charles to Hadley several years before: "My dear Ernest, if you are all that those who know you best believe you to be, we are glad to give you our heart's treasure into your keeping."[25]

The Benevolence of "Uncle Gus"

Pauline looked for a place for the newlyweds to live in Paris. She found a spacious apartment at 6 rue Ferou near the Luxembourg Gardens that took in the morning sunlight and had plenty of rooms for family and work. The monthly rent was 900 francs (which they could afford) but the down payment was the equivalent of $3,000 (which they could not).[26] Uncle Gus came to the rescue.

Henry and Annie Pfeiffer had no children. Gus and Louise lost their only child in infancy. Their love and affection was poured out on their nieces and nephews (recall that these brothers were three of 10 children). Paul and Mary's children were the only children in their immediate vicinity, and Pauline Pfeiffer was a favorite of her Uncle Gus. After Henry died in 1939, Gus ran the family companies.

Pauline's trust fund originally was precisely the same as Hadley's—$60,000.[27] This produced a monthly income of about $250—about the same amount as Ernest and Hadley lived on in their early Paris years. Pauline (and therefore Hemingway) owed everything to the largesse of Uncle Gus. This he was glad to give because of his "love and affection" for his dear niece and his "desire to share the prosperity which has come to us," so that Pauline could "better and more successfully evolve your personality and attain your hopes and ideals."[28] Ernest dedicated *A Farewell to Arms* not to his new wife but rather to Uncle Gus.

There was also a later trust fund dated Feb. 18, 1930, that came through City Bank Farmers Trust Company of New York in the names of both Ernest and Pauline, likely again money from Uncle Gus. There was yet another trust set up on Nov. 2, 1936, this time for Ernest himself. The base value is not known, but in 1938, Gus provided 22 shares of William R. Warner stock valued at $100 per share each to be held by Ernest in his trust.[29]

John Dos Passos, who suggested Key West to Hemingway as early as 1921, was instrumental in the newlyweds' eventual move to Florida. "Dos," as Ernest called him, married Katy Smith in 1929. He said Key West was truly an island that "smelt of the Gulf Stream"—it was linked to Havana by ferry and attracted a diverse population that was part Spanish, part Cuban, as well as an English-speaking population from the East Coast.[30]

In 1930, Ernest and Pauline headed back there from Paris via Cuba, and Uncle Gus promised to have a new yellow Ford runabout waiting for them.[31] The car was late, though, and Ernest and Pauline were forced to wait for a couple weeks. They fell in love with Key West and decided to make Florida their new home.

The house at 907 Whitehead St. in Key West (now the Hemingway Home and Museum) was a gift from Uncle Gus in 1931.[32] The purchase came after Gus took a vacation in Key West to see Pauline and little Patrick. She showed it to him, with the asking price of $8,000, and Gus was ready with the cash to buy it on the spot for his favorite niece.[33] For the first time, Ernest Hemingway had a house in the United States. Once planted in Key West, though, Ernest looked for new experiences in far away places. A home to him was "a place...to come back to."[34]

The next year, 1932, Uncle Gus financed a chartered deep-sea fishing trip for himself, Hemingway and some friends to the Dry

Library of Congress HABS FLA-179-2; public domain

*The house at **907 Whitehead Street in Key West** about 1933, purchased by **Uncle Gus** for his favorite niece and her husband. When their marriage disintegrated, Pauline said to Ernest, "I'll keep the house." The house is a prominent museum today.*

Tortugas, 70 miles from Key West in the Gulf of Mexico. A storm marooned them for a bit and everyone got to see Ernest's temper on display.[35]

Then, after returning to Key West, Ernest got into a fight with Archibald MacLeish—an old friend who took him in after he separated from Hadley. MacLeish was a prize-winning playwright of some distinction who became the Librarian of Congress a few years later.

MacLeish said Ernest's ego needed to be pricked and Ernest replied that MacLeish's prick was not big enough to do the job. MacLeish stormed out of the Key West house, found a hotel, and took the first flight back to New York.[36] It's unclear if all this took place in front of Uncle Gus in the house he had just purchased. MacLeish got over it and, if it were an issue, Uncle Gus did too.

In 1932, Hemingway decided he would go on safari in East Africa. Adding up the cost of transatlantic travel, high-end accommodations for the trip, hunting permits, and a Great White Hunter like Philip Percival to lead the way, the total excursion was approaching $22,000 (about $325,000 in today's dollars). Not to worry: Gus was ready.[37] The trip was postponed until the end of 1933. Early on, Ernest picked up dysentery and spent weeks recuperating instead of hunting. His Key West friend, Charles Thompson, bagged more animals than Ernest, but Ernest's mind gathered material for multiple stories.

Meanwhile, Hemingway's books were becoming more popular and honors started coming in. Cyril Clemens, a descendant of Samuel Clemens's relations who lived in the St. Louis suburbs of Webster Groves and Kirkwood, invited Ernest to be an honorary vice president of the Mark Twain Society—which he "accepted with 'great pleasure'."[38] When Ernest decided it was time get a boat of his own, he was reluctant to ask Uncle Gus. Instead, he cobbled together a combination of publishing advances and royalty payments to make the purchase. Uncle Gus joined Ernest on subsequent fishing trips, including one in May 1935 when Ernest pulled in a record-setting 381-pound tuna. Uncle Gus was thrilled to witness it.[39]

But Gus's attitude started to change around 1937. When Gus had to cancel a trip, Ernest responded with a telegram saying that it was OK because he wouldn't have to come home, now that the trip was postponed.[40] Whether serious or joking, Ernest's message upset Uncle Gus. He replied, "I hope...the happiness your return [gives] to Pauline and the boys is worth the trip back."[41]

In 1938, Uncle Gus and Aunt Louise made a trip to Key West. Ernest and Uncle Gus went out fishing while Pauline and Aunt Louise enjoyed being at home. Ernest was distracted, Gus was exhausted, and stormy weather made the trip more subdued than enjoyable.[42]

Storm clouds were also gathering at the Hemingway home. Ernest's marriage to Pauline was starting to fail. They put on pretenses for their visitors/benefactors. On the last day of Uncle Gus's visit, during dinner, the lights went out.[43] There could have been no clearer omen for the end of Ernest's relationship with the Pfeiffers.

Uncle Gus took much pleasure in helping his favorite niece and he was thrilled by her marriage to the great Hemingway. His generosity and support were deep, and he empowered them to afford an exceptional lifestyle. His mantra was to "give such financial aid as may be necessary to enable each to live in accordance with his station in life, without lessening individual effort and development."[44] Ernest shared his life with Pauline in this chapter, but that lifestyle was enabled entirely by Gus Pfeiffer and the success of the Pfeiffer Chemical Company.

Blame for a Mother's Death

Ernest and Pauline had made one earlier visit to Key West. They left Paris early in April 1928, returning to the States for the birth of their child. When they arrived in Key West, Pauline was six months pregnant with the baby who turned out to be Patrick Hemingway. While there, totally by coincidence, Ernest learned that his father, mother, and uncle were checking on their investment property in St. Petersburg, so Ernest invited them down. Ernest rounded up Pauline and took everyone out to lunch. It was Pauline's first time meeting her in-laws and she turned on the charm, even while knowing the senior Hemingways were not crazy about their son's divorce and remarriage.[45] The lunch was the last time Ernest saw his father—Dr. Clarence Hemingway committed suicide on Dec. 6, 1928.

Charles Thompson, who lived and owned businesses in Key West, guided Ernest's introduction to the island on this visit. During the tour, Thompson took Hemingway to Joe (Josie) Russell's saloon "Sloppy Joe's," which would become the author's iconic hangout.[46]

Pauline and Ernest had planned a trip to Piggott around the birth. For the time being, though, they were planted in Key West and Ernest was in no hurry to leave. Then, friends started arriving—Dos Passos, Katy Smith (soon to be Katy Dos Passos), her brother Bill Smith, and other people old and new. Several of them stayed a month, to Ernest's delight.[47]

But late in May, after a month of partying, Pauline worried about the birth. Paul, "Papa Pfeiffer," came to Key West to check on his daughter during the month of mirth. Everyone became concerned about the wisdom of making a car journey half way across the country with a woman in her eighth month of pregnancy. Pauline took a train to Piggott on May 20; Ernest and Paul would drive the car.[48]

Ernest wrote to his father for advice, asking if Dr. Hemingway had recommendations for a hospital in Petoskey, Mich., near their summer home, and maybe hiring a nurse and cook for Windemere cottage. His father, an obstetrician, said St. Louis or Kansas City would be a much better choice. Clarence also said they could come to Oak Park and he would handle the birth himself.[49]

The choice was Kansas City.

Papa Pfeiffer, who had been skeptical of the marriage, hoped he could get to know Hemingway man-to-man on the trip. But, their relationship remained rocky in Key West and on one occasion he became enraged when Ernest flirted with a waitress at dinner.

Still, they had a drive across the South and hot nights in tourist cabins to work it out. According to Pfeiffer biographer Ruth Hawkins, by the time they arrived in Piggott at the end of May, they had forged an "uneasy alliance"—noting "Ernest did not take kindly to Piggott and Piggott did not take kindly to Ernest."[50]

The decision to go to Kansas City, some 400 miles north of Piggott, was a tough one—the birth was extremely difficult. Patrick Miller Hemingway was delivered by cesarean section on June 28, 1928, a very risky birth for Pauline, whose health was fragile. As of this writing, Patrick is still living in Bozeman, Mont.

Pauline was told not to have any more children, but as a Catholic, she refused any kind of birth control. Son Gregory Hancock Hemingway was born by cesarean section on Nov. 12, 1931, again in Kansas City.[51] Gregory, like Patrick, was largely raised by a nanny

Library of Congress HABS FLA-179-12; public domain

Ernest, Gregory, and Patrick *caught by the photographer in what looks like an accidental photo. The 1933 image was taken as part of the Historic American Buildings Survey of the Key West house conducted by New Deal photographers. Called the Tift House, the building was a significant landmark before Pauline and Ernest ever lived there.*

and left in the care of others, while Pauline supported her husband in his adventures as she promised.

Gregory, known as Gigi, had significant emotional problems. He married at 19 and both he and his wife Shirley worked in Los Angeles for the Douglas Aircraft Co., later part of St. Louis-based McDonnell-Douglas. Gigi drank heavily and abused drugs. He was secretly a cross-dresser and was arrested on Sept. 30, 1951, for entering a women's restroom in drag and high on drugs.[52]

Pauline, meanwhile, suffered frequent headaches[53] and showed signs of emotional distress several times during her marriage to Ernest.[54] When Gregory was arrested—more than a decade after her divorce from Ernest—Pauline was living in San Francisco with her sister Jinny and Jinny's lover Laura Archera, who in 1956 became the wife of Aldous Huxley.[55]

When her son was arrested, Pauline rushed to Los Angeles and tried to help. Gregory suggested it would be best if Ernest were not told of the arrest. Pauline replied, "Yes...a lot of things would be simpler if you had only one parent."[56]

So, Pauline called Ernest and told him what happened. He exploded. She delayed a longer conversation until she returned to Jinny and Laura's home in San Francisco. Impatient, Ernest phoned her there and what started as reasonable conversation erupted into yelling and screaming. A better mother, said Ernest, would have been less permissive and none of this would have happened.[57] Jinny and Laura recalled Pauline went to bed in tears after the call. They were awakened by Pauline's "horrendous screams" early in the morning.[58]

She was taken to St. Vincent's Hospital in San Francisco where she underwent exploratory surgery to try to find the source of what she described as extreme pain. Her blood pressure, always too high, skyrocketed then dropped. The shock caused her death on the operating table. It was 4 a.m. on Oct. 1, 1951. She was 56 years old.[59] (The autopsy attributed the spike to a tumor in the adrenal gland.)

Gregory was still in jail at 9 a.m. that morning. Gregory called Jinny for details, but she would share none. Jinny blamed Ernest for Pauline's death. When Ernest tried to find out what happened she was silent. Rather than send Pauline's remains to Key West or Piggott, Jinny decided to bury her in Hollywood. She felt a Catholic funeral was out of the question since Pauline was divorced, so Jinny purchased a plot in the Memorial Park Cemetery (now Hollywood Forever Cemetery) on Santa Monica Boulevard next to Paramount Studios.

Only five people attended the graveside service: Jinny and Laura, Gregory, a friend Jay McAvoy, and favorite cousin Garfield Merner. Patrick was in Africa and could not return home in time. Pauline's parents were both dead. Uncle Gus still lived in New York but couldn't get there in time. Ernest was not invited and not welcome. She was buried apart from her family. Instead, she lay near Cecil B. DeMille, Marion Davies, and Tyrone Powers.[60] Aunty Laura's California brother, Leonard Merrill, was buried there in 1939, and Jinny would be too in 1973.

A few months after Pauline's burial, Gregory, then 20, used money from his inheritance to visit his father, by then living in Cuba, accompanied by his wife and daughter. Some time had passed and Gregory brought up the subject of his arrest.

"It wasn't so bad, really, Papa," he said.

"No?! It killed Mother!"[61] Ernest exclaimed.

That accusation crippled Gregory emotionally for decades. He eventually was able to complete medical school and became a doctor like his grandfather. Unfortunately, his demons of chemical dependency and repressed sexual struggle led to major problems.

Forty-four years after the cross-dressing incident, in 1995, he began gender-reassignment surgery, aiming to transition to a woman, Gloria. The surgery wasn't completely successful and he had some of it reversed. In 2001, he was arrested for indecent exposure while impaired and died on October 1st in the Women's Detention Center in Miami-Dade County—50 years to the day from when his mother died on the operating table.

The Beginning of the End

Ernest sat in Sloppy Joe's on a December afternoon in 1936. In walked three travellers from St. Louis: Edna Gellhorn, son Alfred, and daughter Martha.[62] They came there by bus from Miami on a lark to see the Keys and were intrigued by an establishment named "Sloppy Joe's." Ernest hunched over the bar, a large dirty man in shorts and a grubby T-shirt.[63] He turned on the charm for the new guests and when he learned they were from St. Louis, he found plenty to talk about.

Ernest Hemingway had just met his third wife.

John F. Kennedy Library EHPH05598

Ernest and Martha *after their Wyoming marriage in 1940. It brought to a close, said Martha, three years of "living in contented sin."*

4

The Gellhorn Family

"St. Louis has taught me all I know, and I'm leaving."

Martha Gellhorn

attributed by her friend Mary Taussig Hall

One of the great associations America has with Ernest Hemingway is his Cuban estate. The *Finca Vigia* was home base for his rowdy adventure on the Caribbean and the setting for perhaps his greatest story, *The Old Man and the Sea.* He was a regular on the island for many years; his permanent residence there was his gift to share with his third St. Louis wife, Martha Gellhorn. It was Martha, though, who found it, cleaned it up, and convinced Ernest it was the place for him.

A Chance Meeting in Key West

Ernest was nursing a drink while reading his mail at Sloppy Joe's bar in December 1936 when three tourists from St. Louis entered: the recently-widowed Edna Gellhorn, her youngest son Alfred (a medical student at Washington University in St. Louis), and her vivacious daughter Martha. Upon introduction, they quickly established their St. Louis connections. They fell into a long conversation and lingered at the bar, enjoying a run of Ernest's favorite drink—the "Doble"—roughly a daiquiri with twice the alcohol, none of the sugar, blended with the juices of limes and grapefruit.

Ernest instantly was smitten with Martha and grew to adore Edna. Martha was sleek, smart, and elegant—and looked very different from the other women he pursued. Edna was shrewd, gay, and open—she would be the mother figure he never had.[1]

His wife Pauline, meanwhile, was getting angry waiting at their Key West home with dinner guests Charles and Lorene Thompson, old and dear friends. Charles went off to fetch Ernest from the bar where he found Ernest holding court with the Gellhorns. Ernest refused to leave. Charles reported back to Pauline, "He's talking to a beautiful blond in a black dress."[2] Hemingway had just met his third wife.

Theising Collection; public domain

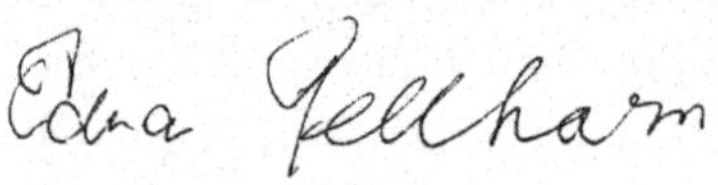

***Edna Gellhorn** press photo, about 1920. She was the loving mother Ernest never had. She made a surprise visit before Martha and Ernest's wedding in an attempt to stop the marriage.*

The friendship between Hemingway and the Gellhorns ripened quickly. After New Year's Day, Edna and Alfred left Key West for St. Louis. But Martha stayed behind, checking into the Colonial Hotel for another week of Florida sun and surf. Ernest accompanied her around Key West while she remained, to the point where Pauline surmised, "I suppose Ernest is busy again helping Miss Gellhorn with her writing."[3]

Martha spent plenty of time in the Key West house with Ernest and Pauline, to the point she felt like a fixture there. She adored the Hemingway sons and was fond of Pauline as a mother. Martha finally left Florida Jan. 10, 1937, for her long journey back to St. Louis.

Ernest quickly declared he had business in New York and set off for Miami, catching up there with Martha. They met at a restaurant in Miami where they dined under the chaperoning of boxer Tom Heeney. Then they shared a train as far north as Jacksonville.[4]

Once back in St. Louis, Martha wrote to Pauline and acknowledged the dinner with Ernest and Heeney in Miami. She said how much she admired Ernest's collected works. She included two photos of her husband, Bertrand, as if to disarm Pauline's concern about Ernest's attraction.[5] "Whatever Pauline's opinion of this letter," wrote biographer Carlos Baker, "it must have struck her as curiously reminiscent of some of those that she herself had sent to Hadley" in 1926. She was far too perceptive not to notice.[6]

Meanwhile, Ernest had become disenchanted with Pauline. He made it public in August 1936 with the publication of his short story "The Snows of Kilimanjaro." In the story, the lead character, Philip, recounts the places he's been and they are the same places Ernest and Pauline had been. Ernest makes his intentions clear when Philip says that where he goes now, he goes alone.[7]

Martha was the catalyst for the end of Ernest's second marriage. When time for the divorce came years later, Pauline said bluntly, "I'll keep the house."[8] Ernest was glad to be free of it all.

Martha said publicly at a Des Moines speaking event about this same time that her own marriage was "all washed up."[9] So both Ernest and Martha were in marriages that were ending when they had their first encounter. Some wonder if Martha had planned it this way all along.

A Woman of St. Louis and a Citizen of the World

Martha's mother was Edna Fischel Gellhorn. Edna was born in St. Louis on Dec. 18, 1878. Edna's parents, Washington and Martha (Ellis) Fischel, were early founders of the Ethical Society in St. Louis, for which the acoustically perfect Sheldon Concert Hall was built in 1912.[10] Edna married George Gellhorn, the city's first obstetrician/gynecologist. He had studied under Edna's father and stayed in St. Louis at his father-in-law's insistence.

Edna was an early advocate of women's suffrage and helped establish the League of Women Voters. When George saw how poorly illustrated the anatomy textbooks were at his daughter's school, he pushed Edna to create a better school. Together, George and Edna were among the founding parents of the John Burroughs School in 1923, with annual fees of $1,000 (or about $14,000 in 2019, though the fees have increased to about $30,000). Martha was pulled from Mary Institute (alma mater of Hadley Richardson and Katy Smith) and enrolled in the first class at Burroughs.[11]

In the Gellhorn house racial slurs were not tolerated, nor were ethnic smears, gossip, or discussions of money. The children were asked to base opinions on observations. *Robert's Rules of Order* governed family discussions and disputes were settled with reference books.[12] Martha loved facts and open-mindedness, yet as a teenager, Martha disliked St. Louis and dreamed of living in France to see the places her father reminisced about.[13]

Theising photo

***The Gellhorn House** at 4366 McPherson in the lovely Central West End of St. Louis. Martha called the housing on her street "unbearably ugly." Hemingway stayed here on May 22-23, 1941, on his way home from the China trip.*

Martha enjoyed her family home at 4366 McPherson Ave., but concluded the housing along the posh street was "unbearably ugly" and that the nearby Catholic cathedral had "hideous" decoration (perhaps referring to the all-mosaic walls inside.)

William Julius Polk, a Mullanphy descendant who lived at the historic *Taille de Noyer* house in Florissant, was a Fortnightly Club friend of Martha Gellhorn. The club, he said, "was an exercise in deportment and ballroom behavior," noting that its rules rubbed against her "slightly rebellious and slightly nonconformist" nature. "When we were growing up, we felt that St. Louis was somewhat midwestern and provincial, and she thought it would be more interesting to belong to the big world."[14]

Martha may have been inclined to leave St. Louis sooner than she did had she not been so attached to her mother Edna. From her, Martha received (and returned) lifelong love. From her father, she received the gift of curiosity and a taste for excellence, though she struggled emotionally to meet his standard for excellence.

Edna and Martha would visit Creve Coeur Lake on Saturdays with a picnic of sandwiches and lemonade, and a volume of Browning poetry that they would take turns reciting.[15] It was inevitable that Martha would leave St. Louis—there was nothing in the city she needed and plenty in the outside world she wanted.

She headed off to Bryn Mawr College but decided in 1929, like Hadley Richardson did, to drop out and seek her future in France. Hadley had dropped out of the same college in 1912 and later followed Ernest to Paris. Gellhorn had been to Europe already—her father took her and her brother, Alfred, to his birthplace in Germany.

Arriving in Paris at age 21, she embraced her freedom away from the confines of home. She also embraced the already-married Bertrand de Jouvenel. Bertrand was seduced as a teenager by his stepmother, the French writer Colette, and they had an affair that lasted five years. He was married with a child when he met Martha in 1930. Martha spent 10 months in France and they became lovers, despite his marriage. Martha returned to St. Louis in December 1930 alone, noting in her diary that she was "ill and pregnant." She traveled to Chicago for an abortion.[16]

Bertrand wrote to Edna from France to make a plea for Martha, who was ailing and unhappy. He said she was sick because of her loneliness—caused by the distance from him and the emotional distance from her parents (at least her father). His solution was for Martha to return to "stable" and "enduring" France rather than be forced to stay in St. Louis, which did not satisfy her intellectual curiosity.[17]

Martha "married" Bertrand de Jouvenel over the summer of 1933 in Spain. They held a ceremony at the home of portrait painter

Jose Maria Sert and his artist-wife who had just completed a sculpture of Martha. Bertrand's wife Marcelle refused to divorce him and Martha always questioned the legality of their marriage in Spain.[18] The marriage was announced and published in the *St. Louis Post-Dispatch*, confirmed at the time by Edna, and even mentioned one of Martha's public speeches, but there was never a divorce before she married Ernest.

MARRIED IN SPAIN

Ashen-Brenner Photo.

The former Miss Martha Ge
horn, daughter of Dr. and M
George Gellhorn, 4366 McPhers
avenue, whose marriage to Be
rand de Jouvenel of Paris
Spain last summer was announc
today.

Newspapers.com; public domain

***Martha's** wedding announcement in the St. Louis Star, Nov. 4, 1933. The marriage was a sham but Edna confirmed it to reporters.*

Bertrand visited St. Louis in July 1934. He was curious about his wife's birthplace and wanted to meet her parents. Martha Love Symington, a close friend of Martha, gave Bertrand a tour of the city. When the car stopped at "Holy Corners" at Kingshighway and Washington, not far from the Gellhorn home, Symington explained the four faiths that built the edifices at and around the intersection: Temple Israel, St. John's Methodist Church, Second Baptist Church, and the First Church of Christ Scientist.

Bertrand, from Catholic France, peppered her with questions about these houses of worship. Symington recalled, "Here was this sophisticated Frenchman and he did not seem to have any idea of these splits in the Church," she noted, "as if he had never heard of the Reformation."[19]

Through Edna's work in the suffrage movement, Martha met Eleanor Roosevelt. Martha got a New Deal agency job documenting the living conditions of Americans across the country. She traveled by train around the United States to witness the Great Depression through the eyes of working families. She was invited to a White House dinner in 1935, to which the unconventional Martha wore a black sweater and skirt. Eleanor Roosevelt (hard of hearing and prone to loud speaking) bellowed to her husband, "talk to that child on your left; she says that all the people in the South have pellagra or syphilis." Table conversation stopped and laughter erupted. Martha was furious and was ready to storm away from the table, but soon realized the gift she had just been given. The President engaged her in conversation, was impressed by her knowledge, and invited her for another visit to discuss these matters she found so important.[20]

Still, Martha bristled in the hierarchy and opulence of the White House while the rest of the country tried to survive the Depression. Eleanor was concerned that Martha, the rebellious fighter for social justice, might alienate the very people who could help her cause.[21] Even so, Martha grew closer to Eleanor, loving her as a second mother. She did not, however, feel the same way about the President.

Martha's father, George Gellhorn, died in January 1936, while she was home in St. Louis ill with anemia. The next month, she wrote to Eleanor Roosevelt and asked for help in getting a job in New York. St. Louis, it seemed, "specialized in women who sold dresses in fashionable stores" and was once again too confining to suit her.[22] The First Lady responded to her request and made some arrangements to help Martha. In fact, she invited her to stay as a guest in the White House for a time to get back on her feet.

Eleanor opened the door for Martha to meet H. G. Wells—long a literary giant. He was married with children, but had notorious affairs. Martha, too, was still "married" but by this time had grown disenchanted with Bertrand. In June 1936, she met Wells in England and saw a great opportunity for his advice and support.

Gellhorn became his lover despite a great age difference (he was 70, she not even 30).[23] Wells endorsed Martha's work, secured British publication of her book, and remarked fondly of his love for her in his memoirs. Martha, to the contrary, never acknowledged the affair, described him as an intellectual bully, and described the relationship as a "vague crush."[24]

During this time Martha produced *The Trouble I've Seen*, her first successful book and in which H. G. Wells wrote the preface. Eleanor Roosevelt talked up the book in her nationally syndicated newspaper column and there were rave reviews in *The New York Times* and the *Saturday Review*. The country loved her book and Martha Gellhorn became a nationally (even internationally) respected writer.[25] It was dedicated to her father, who did not live long enough to see its publication.

Later in 1936, Martha began a brief love affair with Allen Grover, a business writer from St. Louis who worked with her at *Time* magazine in New York. Their families were members of the same country club. His father was

Newspapers.com; public domain

***George Gellhorn** obituary photo, 1936. The family took a vacation several months later to console themselves, arriving in Key West and bumping into Ernest Hemingway.*

James H. Grover, president of the St. Louis Union Trust Company, and the family lived at 5061 Lindell Boulevard in one of the grand homes facing Forest Park. Allen, years later, liked to tell the story that he got in trouble as a second grader for kissing St. Louisan Dorothy Walker—the mother of President George H. W. Bush.[26]

Not surprisingly, Allen already was married. His wife Beatrice Beard Grover was an artist of note, whose work is collected in the Whitney Museum. Martha and Allen encouraged each other professionally and enjoyed each other's company, but Martha soon pulled away when she felt the relationship getting one-sided. However, a friendship between the two lasted.[27]

When Martha met Ernest in December 1936 in Key West, she had just broken off with Allen and was riding the peak of her successful career thus far. She was 28, and was experienced enough to realize she was ready to catapult to the next level—and that Ernest Hemingway could take her there.

Martha returned to St. Louis at the end of January. Ernest was off to Spain to cover the Spanish Civil War and Martha longed to follow him. Once again, she had her fill of St. Louis, and in mid-March of 1937 she took a knapsack, fifty dollars, and the clothes on her back, and headed to Barcelona.[28]

She was not happy in St. Louis and quick to leave. Yet, in times of trouble during her life, she would return to St. Louis for its stability, its familiarity, and its reliability.

Finding the *Finca Vigia*

Martha and her colleague Sidney Franklin caught up with Ernest in Valencia, Spain, in 1937. Ernest greeted her with "I knew you'd get here, daughter, because I fixed it so you could." Enraged because Ernest in fact had done nothing, Martha gritted her teeth and let it pass.[29] Getting down to business, she found the man she was following and was excited to be reporting from a war zone.

The love affair between Ernest and Martha began on this trip. It fit her pattern, a pattern one of her biographers referred to as hero searching. Martha would find married men whom she admired, would connect personally and professionally with them, and—when they no longer held hero status in her eyes—she would leave them. That's what was ahead for Ernest, but during the Spanish Civil War, all was new and exciting.

The physical relationship between the two was exposed when a mortar shell exploded in the boiler room at the Hotel Florida where they were sleeping together. Fellow journalist Tom Delmer reported how interesting it was to see "all kinds of liaisons" exposed as hotel occupants "poured from their bedrooms to seek shelter in the basement," including Ernest and Martha.[30]

When his 45-day reporting assignment in Spain ended, Ernest went to Paris and renewed his many friendships there before heading home to New York and then on to Key West. Martha traveled to Washington to see the Roosevelts and there she arranged a meeting between FDR and the press covering the Spanish Civil War that Ernest attended.[31] During this time, Ernest's novel *To Have and Have Not* was released to mixed reviews that made Ernest upset.

Pauline made one last attempt to save her marriage at the end of 1937. It had been a year since Ernest met Martha at Sloppy Joe's and during that year she grew her hair out long like Martha's, just as she cut her hair a decade before to resemble Hadley's. Ernest was back in Europe and Pauline made a hasty trip to Paris, only to discover Ernest and Martha were in Spain enjoying a Catalonian Christmas.

Pauline began pulling strings to get a wartime visa for Spain but Ernest returned to Paris where they stayed together at the Hotel du Rond-Point des Champs-Elysees at the heart of Paris.[32] Bill Bird, an old friend and publisher of Hemingway's first book, paid them a visit and recalled the gloomy atmosphere. He said later they quarreled furiously over Martha.

By now, Ernest was in a terrible frame of mind and picked arguments everywhere. He yelled at his editor, Max Perkins, for not advertising *To Have and Have Not* enough. He vilified other authors (Max Eastman, Tom Wolfe, Scott Fitzgerald) in letters to publishers, even slamming their own praise of him. He was torn between going back to the war in Spain to gather more material or going back to Key West to write-up what he already had.[33] The petulance, the indecisiveness, the arguing—they were all bubbling up from his core distress around his fully exposed affair with Martha. He went home to Key West briefly through March 1938, but the restless man soon headed back to Spain for yet another assignment.

By November 1938, Ernest was in New York with Pauline and his sons at her apartment on East 50th Street, keeping up appearances. The lease on the apartment was ending, and the two parents traveled separately back to Key West.[34] By Valentine's Day 1939, Ernest was in Havana writing and the permanent physical separation from Pauline had begun.

Ernest adored the Caribbean, and especially the island of Cuba. His original headquarters in Havana was the Hotel Ambos Mundos, where in his favorite room he could write and run his life and career. He had a standing reservation.

Theising photo

The placard outside the ***Hotel Ambos Mundos*** *in Havana. It was for years Ernest's headquarters while in Cuba and he had a standing reservation there. Ernest loved it; Martha hated it.*

Arriving in April 1939, Martha liked the routine of Cuba; writing all the morning hours into the early afternoon, spending late afternoons playing tennis, swimming or fishing, and enjoying evenings in the island's splendid restaurants. However, dessert was where the mutual enjoyment came to a close.

Hemingway could spend hours at the bars and clubs. She didn't go along. His room was full of fishing gear and a beat-up typewriter. She couldn't work there. He was sloppy. She was ordered and fastidious. He loved hotel life. She hated it. Ernest promised to find a house for them, but it was Martha who found a real estate agent and started looking for a place to rent.[35]

She found it 20 minutes outside Havana, a roomy one-story house sitting on a neglected old farm with a nice view called *Finca Vigia*—"Lookout Farm." There was a swimming pool, extensive landscaping, and tennis courts, but all in need of immediate attention.[36]

Martha showed the place to Ernest and his first reaction was that the rent was too high and the place too dilapidated.[37] He left for a fishing trip and while he was gone Martha used her own money to execute the lease. She hired painters, a carpenter, two gardeners, and a cook. When Ernest returned from his fishing trip, he was astounded at the transformation and moved in right away.[38] They were becoming established as a couple.

Meanwhile, many around Ernest wondered why he needed to divorce Pauline at all. Martha was not pushing for marriage and Ernest was concerned about Pauline's health. Both of them were in a good place, Martha writing fiction again and Ernest productive between fishing adventures. *Finca Vigia* offered them comfort and creative space, all for $100 a month (about $1,800 today).[39]

Edna arrived at *Finca Vigia* July 21, 1939—just in time for Ernest's 40th birthday party. They enjoyed lavish meals at home over the subsequent days and Ernest gave Edna a tour of Havana, where they enjoyed drinks and dinner. Martha read to Edna excerpts of her latest book, *A Stricken Field*, and they discussed Spain for hours. Ernest read excerpts of *For Whom the Bell Tolls* and Edna enjoyed the literary evenings with her daughter and Ernest Hemingway.[40]

Throughout this time Edna and Ernest bonded, and Martha believed Ernest truly loved her mother. Ernest's brother Leicester thought Edna could see deeply into a person's character but never intrude.[41] Edna summed up Ernest carefully and told Martha she felt sorry for him.

Martha was shocked by her mother's observation—after all, Hemingway was a famously robust man who had achieved greatness. Edna dropped the point. Later, Martha realized her mother sensed the great emotional instability that wasn't yet apparent on the surface of the 40-year-old author.[42]

As Hitler became more aggressive in Europe, Martha wrote Eleanor Roosevelt more often, making clear her opposition to Hitler and the Nazi Party. Martha wrote a piece on Nazi subversion in Cuba in 1940 as she saw the rise of fascism among German and Spanish aliens on the island. She explored the fifth-column sympathizers and talked to many VIPs on the island, yet *Collier's* ultimately rejected her piece. Martha was disappointed but looked toward the future and was eager to go on assignment in Europe again—perhaps in November after they took a trip to the American West.[43]

A Marriage of Equals

Martha was *so* different from Hadley and Pauline. Ernest's first two wives were boyish in style and stature; Martha was a tall beauty queen with flowing blond hair. When they met, Martha was an accomplished and experienced writer; Hadley did not have a career and Pauline was just beginning hers. Martha came out of a wealthy St. Louis family just like Hadley and Pauline, but Martha successfully made her own way, living off her writing career. Ernest, too, by the time he met Martha, was generating his own income and no longer lived off a wife's trust fund or a rich uncle's generosity. Here he was faced with a marriage of equals and Ernest was unsure how to handle it.

At the end of October 1940, Martha was ill with the flu but Ernest was excited about their upcoming trip, a camping trip out West where they would hike 23 miles on a rough trail through the wilderness. Martha liked the way the pending trip calmed his drinking and that he saw it as a "tonic." Never mind the flu—they were getting married.

The couple went to Sun Valley, Idaho, a location that would figure prominently in Ernest's later life. Imagine their surprise when Edna Gellhorn showed up unannounced. She had traveled across the country to stop their impending marriage.

Martha had heard all the arguments before, but Ernest had not. He was hurt by Edna's analysis of his character, and felt wounded by the motherly woman he adored more than his own. Ernest noticed Martha was still going through with the wedding, although she was not an eager bride.[44]

The wedding took place before a Justice of the Peace on Nov. 21, 1940, in the dining room of the Union Pacific station in Cheyenne, Wyo. Martha was 32 years old and Ernest, 41. Roasted moose was served for the wedding dinner.[45]

Word of the Western marriage spread quickly. Mary Taussig Hall, Martha's friend from St. Louis, expressed her happiness to Edna. Edna replied, "Well, we'll see. Don't get too happy too soon."[46] Scott Fitzgerald, who would die one month later, said he found it odd for Ernest to marry "a really attractive woman," noting that his pattern had been "his Pygmalion-like creations."[47] Even Martha secretly had doubts. The marriage, she said, brought to an end three years of "living in contented sin."[48]

Meanwhile, Pauline, relieved that the tension in her house was over, sent a note to Hemingway's mother Grace in Chicago tell-

Theising Collection

*The **Union Pacific Railroad Station** in Cheyenne, Wyoming. Ernest and Martha were married in the dining room there in November 1940. Roasted moose was served for dinner that evening.*

ing her about the divorce from Ernest. She told Grace that Ernest followed his heart. She compared Ernest's heart to a dark forest and said it was miraculous when "people did anything right in this world, considering what they had to contend with." Those words—"the heart of another is a dark forest"—became the epigraph of Martha's short story collection two months later.[49]

Ernest and Martha dedicated their 1940 publications, *For Whom the Bell Tolls* and *A Stricken Field,* to each other. They went from Wyoming to New York, where reporters surrounded them. Martha likened it to a "runaway elevator" ride.

Martha used her connections there and arranged a meeting between Hemingway and H. G. Wells. She was hoping for a rousing encounter, but it fizzled when Ernest "showed no interest in witty conversation."[50]

That Christmas, Ernest's present to themselves was *Finca Vigia,* a $12,500 gift (just over $225,000 today).[51] For the very first time, Ernest owned his own home.

Martha was torn. She loved *Finca Vigia.* She loved the surroundings, the view, and the relaxed, natural setting. Yet Gellhorn loved travel and adventure. Ernest was not always a willing companion. She wanted to go to China and Ernest reluctantly went along. War was raging in Europe, and it was Martha who wanted to go, becoming more adventurous than Ernest.

Living as a married couple in the Cuba house, Ernest's anger became more and more commonplace. Once he started raging at home, anything could happen. Ernest would hurl objects in the house, shoot out a window, or embarrass his guests. Martha bought cheap drinking glasses so Ernest wouldn't break her family's crystal against the wall.

In June 1941, Ernest's son Gregory visited and witnessed the rage. "I'll show you, you conceited bitch," Ernest yelled at Martha in front of the boy. "They'll be reading my stuff long after the worms have finished with you."[52] When Martha's *Time* magazine friends from New York came for a visit, wearing their pressed flannels and playing perfect tennis, Ernest intentionally mixed-in his coarse local friends who knew nothing of finery or rules.[53]

Theising photo

Entrance to the ***Finca Vigia*** *outside Havana, Cuba. Martha found the place, rented it, and renovated it with her own money prior to Ernest's purchase in December 1940.*

But it was the war in Europe that provoked the sharpest division between Martha Gellhorn and Ernest Hemingway. Martha was ready to go cover it on the ground. Ernest made arrangements to stay in Cuba.

Then, in what may be the strangest contribution by anyone to the American war effort, Ernest outfitted his fishing boat with guns and military supplies, and began scouting for German submarines in the Gulf Stream with a rag-tag navy of locals. His plan, in all seriousness, was to sidle-up to a raised submarine in his boat, somehow open the hatch, and have two jai-alai players on his crew chuck a large bomb down the conning tower.[54] Ernest saw it as important intelligence work. Martha saw it as grown men playing soldier, and said as much. Ernest was infuriated into his throw-a-glass rage.

Soon after, stories began circulating calling Gellhorn unfaithful. Martha denied the gossip, even as her carefree behavior encouraged it. Her biographer Carl Rollyson says that Cuba eventually became "a corrupting life" for both of them.[55] Ernest lost his daily discipline at *Finca Vigia*, and Martha struggled to write about a place so foreign to her.

While Ernest was on his boat looking for Germans, Martha took an assignment that allowed her to pack her bags. Martha's travel papers were for "Martha Hemingway," but she made it clear to her editors at *Collier's*: her byline would always be "Martha Gellhorn."[56]

Going to War and Ending a Marriage

The beginning of 1944 found Martha covering the war in Europe and Ernest scouting the bars of Havana. Martha felt he was shirking his duties as a war correspondent and decided to "blast him loose" from Cuba.[57] She returned to the U.S. between assignments determined to make something happen.

She got help from the writer Roald Dahl, working at the British Embassy in Washington, to arrange wartime passage to London for Ernest. Dahl assigned Hemingway to cover the British air defense of London for an American magazine. Martha grabbed the assignment for *Collier*'s. Ernest approved of it all and they all met in New York to await passage. They partied in Ernest's customary fashion while they were there.[58]

Martha sailed May 11, taking an empty seat on a munitions ship. Ernest stayed behind to wait for a plane flight. When reminded that May 14 was Mother's Day, he thought of his mother Grace and remarked, "I'll have to send the old bitch a wire." A week later, he flew into London and set up residence at the Dorchester Hotel (fondly called "The Dorch").[59]

Shortly thereafter, he met a young war correspondent for the London *Daily Express* named Mary Welsh. She was married to Noel Monks, a war correspondent who had been sent off to Australia. Petite with close-cropped blonde hair, Mary was the same age as Martha. Mary had arrived in London 1940 and rented a penthouse apartment conveniently located near The Dorch.[60]

After lunch in a very warm restaurant, Mary removed her suit coat to reveal a tight sweater underneath. Someone at the table remarked with her look Mary was bound to attract attention, "like bees to a queen."[61] One of the first bees was Ernest. She had read of his arrival in London, an introduction was made, and Ernest had just met his fourth wife (the only one not from St. Louis).

While Martha was still on the munitions ship, Ernest was living it up in London. One night he partied long into the early morning hours and a drunken companion offered to drive the group home in the blackout conditions of London streets. Just a half-mile away, the car crashed into a water tower. Ernest's head smashed the windshield and his knees jammed into the dashboard. The others were able to walk away with only cuts and bruises.

Hemingway required two-and-a-half hours of procedures and 57 stitches. He suffered a concussion (he would have at least four major ones in his life) and the headaches from it plagued him for months.[62]

Martha arrived in Liverpool, agitated from the smoking ban on the munitions ship. She had heard of the accident and headed to the hospital to meet her husband. She found him in bed, his head covered in bandages like a turban, a long beard down to his chest like a mystic. Martha took one look at him and broke into laughter.

Not surprisingly, Ernest was furious at her lack of sympathy. Her deeper truth, however, was disappointment. She loathed the drinking that put Ernest into such a predicament, and it was just one more example of how he no longer lived up to the fighting-man reputation she had assigned him. Once again, a hero in Martha's world was falling from his pedestal.

Ernest's behavior in London over the next weeks was boorish. The concussion was supposed to keep him from writing and drinking. He obeyed the first command but not the second. Binging, he would engage in faux tough-guy behaviors only he seemed to enjoy. Colleagues found it difficult to watch. Ernest fumed at Martha's "cruel neglect" in not caring for him after his accident.[63] He grew vengeful.

One evening in his room at The Dorch with correspondent Ira Wolfert, Ernest phoned Martha's room one floor above to invite her to dinner. She accepted and headed down to Ernest's room. Meanwhile, Ernest went into the bathroom and undressed. When Martha opened his door, Ernest charged at her naked—Martha dashed away in angry tears.[64]

Ira questioned Ernest's behavior in pulling such a stunt, and Ernest called to apologize and extend another invitation. Martha calmed down and reluctantly accepted the next invitation, but insisted that Ernest and Ira come up to her floor to meet.

On their way upstairs, however, Ernest passed Mary Welsh in the hallway. Hemingway had a sharp turn of heart and an abrupt change in plans. Ernest promptly went off with Mary, leaving Ira to dine with Martha.[65] That most likely was the moment Hemingway's marriage with Gellhorn functionally ended.

The disagreements between Martha and Ernest were postponed, however, by a news event—the D-Day invasion was underway. Provision was made for Ernest to go across with soldiers on one of the landing crafts. Martha, as a woman, had to find her own way to Normandy.

Still healing from the accident just two weeks before, Ernest worried about the climb down the net ladders on the side of the transport ship to board the landing craft. Sensing the liability of a crippled observer, commanders changed his assignment to a different transport. He was hoisted aboard swinging in a bosun's chair, so that he could watch the action from the deck. This visible display of his physical weakness (before an audience of soldiers heading into battle, no less) undoubtedly bothered him. Shortly before sunrise he found the strength needed to descend the net ladder to a landing craft. He was part of the seventh wave of infantry storming Omaha Beach.

As the landing craft got closer, Ernest watched the shoreline with binoculars. Battleship guns were raging from behind him. The craft reached France, discharged its load under fire on the second attempt, and left again to pick up survivors and drop Ernest off in a safer place—ensuring that he witnessed the shore but never set foot on it.[66]

Martha, meanwhile, boarded a hospital ship that moved just offshore of the beaches. She witnessed the invasion on June 6 from the ship and actually went on shore the next day to help retrieve the wounded. Ernest took it hard that Martha outperformed him on D-Day. When she made it back to the English side of the Channel, Martha was informed Ernest already had returned to his hotel.

Martha immediately began packing for the Italian front. "I came to see the war, not live in the Dorchester," she said in her good-bye note.[67]

Staying on at The Dorch, Ernest courted Mary Welsh and received visitors. He wrote his required pieces for *Collier's* and followed the RAF action amid the London bombings, but he held back some of his best material for his own use later.[68]

One of the relationships Ernest developed at this time was with Col. Charles Trueman "Buck" Lanham. Ernest finally reached France weeks after D-Day, when he traveled with the 22nd Infantry commanded by Lanham.

Lanham knew the celebrity reporter was being assigned to him and was prepared to dislike Ernest. "Our respect for visitors," said Buck, "diminished in direct proportion to their echelon above our own."[69] He was pleasantly surprised by what he found in Hemingway. Though a famous writer, Ernest was knowledgeable about military information, had an innate sense of battle and terrain, asked intelligent questions, and was quietly deferential.[70] The two built a friendship that would last a lifetime.

By August 1944, the units Ernest was riding with arrived in Paris—a homecoming for Hemingway. Ernest famously "liberated" the Ritz Hotel and held court there. Mary Welsh joined him and he introduced her to his circle of friends, old and new.[71] Ernest stayed there for weeks.

That December, Ernest was at the command center in Rodenbourg watching wire accounts from the Battle of the Bulge nearby in the Ardennes. A military leader there, Lt. Col. John Ruggles, secretly arranged to have Martha come visit Ernest on Christmas Eve. "It was my intention to surprise Ernest pleasantly," he later said, "but I'm afraid it was otherwise." Martha already had raised the prospect of divorce the previous month, and Ernest was still furious with her—calling the visit her "Christmas counterattack."[72]

Apparently Ernest and Martha reconciled enough that night to go to a party together, drive off to Rodenbourg, and spend the night in the same bed. The next morning, Buck Lanham drove them on a tour of the battalion command. Ernest sat up front with Buck rather than in back with Martha.

She argued with him in French, trying to keep their dispute discreet, but Buck understood most everything. She clashed with Ernest over information and story credit.

At a dinner on New Year's Eve, Ernest berated Martha at the table loudly and at length. Friends tried to calm Hemingway, but it didn't work. Finally, people returned to their rooms and an officer reprimanded Ernest for his boorish behavior. Ernest promptly stripped to his long johns, placed a bucket on his head like a helmet, and marched with a mop over his shoulder to Martha's room.[73]

His assignment ended and Ernest returned to the Ritz Hotel in Paris where he resumed his position as celebrity-in-residence (which he shared with the actress Marlene Dietrich, a life-long friendship that began back in 1934). Buck Lanham met Ernest there, and Ernest introduced him to Mary Welsh. Buck presented Ernest with two German machine-gun pistols as souvenirs, as well as plenty of ammunition.

At the table, Ernest passed around a picture of Mary's husband Noel Monks despite Mary's protests. He said Mary's divorce was difficult. He then picked up Noel's photo, walked it over and put it on the fireplace mantle and prepared to shoot it with his new pistol. As he took aim, Buck grabbed his arm, and reminded him of the danger of ricocheting bullets in a crowded dining room.

Ernest went to the restroom. Shots soon rang out and Ernest was giddy with laughter. The photo of Noel was on top of the toilet, riddled with bullet holes. The toilet bowl was shattered and water was flooding not only the restroom and adjacent dining room, but also pouring through the bullet holes into the rooms below.[74]

Martha and Ernest saw each other for the last time in March 1945 at the Dorchester Hotel in London. Ernest met her there on his way back to the United States as the war was ending.

Ernest told her that he was divorcing her in Cuba and Martha made no demands. On Nov. 22, 1945, Ernest sued Martha for divorce. It was one day after their fifth wedding anniversary. The court papers charged her with abandonment of the marriage, and stated that the trouble started in London in 1944. Ernest married Mary Welsh in Cuba in March 1946.[75]

The divorce proved traumatic for Ernest. What had been a marriage of equals became, for him, a marriage of competitors—and he was losing. He took out his vengeance in words. He wrote a nasty poem (never published, but shared) called "To Martha Gellhorn's Vagina." He wrote letters to mutual friends divulging Martha's personal details (some likely exaggerated), describing Martha's body, vilifying her writing, and disparaging her career. He later attacked her character in *Across the River and Into the Trees*. Buck Lanham agreed with Ernest that she was "a bitch from start to finish," but he was appalled by Ernest's animosity toward Martha.[76]

Buck's wife observed that Martha, like Ernest's mother Grace, was one of the few women in Ernest's life who stood up to him. She liked Martha and was sympathetic toward her. Ernest shook his head and recounted his previous marriages—saying Pauline stole him from Hadley, and that when Pauline objected to his love of Martha he told her, "Those who live by the sword must die by the sword."[77]

He took blame for the break-ups of his first two marriages but not the one to Martha. Mrs. Lanham held her tongue. When she later challenged Ernest on his soft opinions toward the Soviet Union, Ernest became enraged and she seemed to take a bit of pride in being admitted to the group of women Ernest Hemingway loathed.[78]

Author and editor Bruce Olson said that Martha Gellhorn may have been the greatest war correspondent of them all. Her career spanned decades and she never shied away from a challenge. Gellhorn biographer Caroline Moorehead remarked that Martha was always looking for a hero. She wanted to experience stability, and she found her father. She wanted to experience France, and she found a Frenchman. She wanted to experience writing, and she found an author. (Hemingway biographer Mary Dearborn quotes Ernest saying to A. E. Hotchner years later: I could not match her in ambition.)

However, Gellhorn failed to play her role for long and the pedestals she created for these men toppled after months or years. She was always more mature in her writing than in her life choices. Losing her sight and terminally ill, she committed suicide in London on Feb. 15, 1998.

Theising Collection

Martha Gellhorn *(1908-1998) was honored on a 42-cent postage stamp in 2008. Ernest was so honored in 1989 with a 25-cent stamp. He probably would be angry that Martha's stamp had a higher denomination, though adjusted for inflation, they were the same and each was the going rate for first-class postage.*

Theising Collection

Aaron Hotchner's *yearbook photo from Soldan High School's The Scrip, 1934.*

5

A. E. Hotchner and an Essay on Sources

"Hotchner simply went along with Hemingway's extravaganzas, thinking, no matter how implausible, they were great entertainment."

Denis Brian, The True Gen (6)

The King of the Hill

Aaron Edward Hotchner was his name, but his byline was "A. E." and he went by "Ed." Hemingway called him "Hotch." He passed away during the writing of this monograph, having lived in Connecticut to age 102. His most recent book came out in 2018. He had been prolific in many areas. It was my pleasure to meet his brother years ago, who lived in their hometown of St. Louis. Selwyn passed away in 2012.

Hotchner was born June 28, 1917. His mother ran a Sunday school program and his father was a jewelry salesman. During the Great Depression, he and his family lived in the Westgate Hotel on Delmar, a street once home to Aunty Charles, all three of the Pfeiffer Brothers, George and Helen Breaker, as well as the Hotchner family.

King of the Hill, Hotchner's fictionalized memoir published in 1972, tells the story of the family's poverty, coping with life in the hotel, the noises and gossip in the hallways. These were the kind of stories Martha Gellhorn collected for Eleanor Roosevelt during the Depression.

Theising Collection

The Westgate Hotel where ***A. E. Hotchner*** *lived during the Great Depression. It was on Delmar (at Kingshighway), which was also the street where the* ***Pfeiffer brothers*** *lived as well as* ***Aunty Laura Charles****.*

Hotchner graduated from Washington University in St. Louis and went on to law school there. When World War II broke out, he joined the Army Air Corps, worked as a journalist and became a major. Afterward, instead of practicing law, he decided to try a career in writing. He got a job with *Cosmopolitan* magazine after the war and promptly dispatched to Cuba to find Ernest Hemingway and convince him to write an essay for the magazine.

It was in 1948 when Hotchner arrived in Havana. He found a room at the Nacional Hotel. He didn't want to go see Hemingway—didn't want to bother the great author—but he had sent a note with the request. He was hoping that Ernest would just say "no" and he could leave. However, it didn't turn out that way. His phone rang.

"This Hotchner?" asked Ernest. "Got your note.... Want to have a drink around five? There's a bar called La Florida. Just tell the taxi."[1] There it was. His life would never be the same.

Ernest arrived late, wearing khaki pants and a white linen shirt, with brown loafers and no socks. He greeted the staff, including the bartender, and everyone was glad to see him. The muscular man approached with outstretched hand—"Hotchner? Welcome to the

Cub Room. Here we have the ultimate achievement of the daiquiri-maker's art." He bragged about downing 16 of them in one night.[2]

Ernest asked where Hotchner was from, lighting up when he heard "St. Louis." "What part? Chouteau Avenue? ...First three wives from St. Louis." Then he added a bit of a sting—"Only good person I know who didn't leave there was Martha Gellhorn's ma."[3] From there, Ernest showed Hotchner how to eat shrimp in the Hemingway style (crunching the heads and tails) and a lifelong friendship was born.

Hotchner became a regular companion: in Havana, at the *Finca Vigia*, traveling Europe, on the *Pilar*, and in Idaho. He was a trusted friend when Ernest began to distrust others. He lined up doctor's appointments and kept track of pills. His 1966 memoir shaped Ernest's legacy unlike any other book.

Hotchner's life work has included biographies, novels, television, and screenplays. His memoirs of growing up in St. Louis during the Depression were chronicled in "King of the Hill," which was made into a 1993 film. He partnered with Paul Newman to create the Newman's Own food product line that donates its profits to charity. He was a significant donor to his alma mater, Washington University in St. Louis, where the Hotchner Theater carries on his work of creative expression.

The Biographies that Shaped Hemingway's Legacy

There are many biographies of Ernest Hemingway, but there are three key works that anchor everything. Anyone looking to understand the author's life should make sure to build her or his knowledge on this foundation.

#1. A. E. Hotchner, *Papa Hemingway: A Personal Memoir*

We know from the study of Martha's marriage to Ernest that he was becoming erratic over time. World War II seemed to mark a transformation—perhaps it was the head injury he suffered, perhaps it was the increased drinking, and perhaps it was just the progression of a natural process. Regardless, Hotchner stood with him during his decline and became the first of

Ernest's biographers to tell the truth about Ernest's illness.

Hotchner told the truth about Ernest's mental decline in his tell-all memoir that wasn't released until five years later. Hemingway's fourth wife, Mary, had worked to manage Ernest's image in the press and keep his incidents quiet. It was well known that Ernest was being treated at the Mayo Clinic, reportedly responding well to electro-shock therapy.

But this wasn't true. Ernest was in decline.

By 1960, Ernest was worried that the Internal Revenue Service and Hoover's FBI were investigating him for tax liabilities and other crimes. A guest staying at his home in Ketchum, Idaho, watched as Ernest obsessed over details—did Immigration ask to check her passport? Did anyone come around asking questions? She must be lying when she said no—they bought her off. She's gone over to them. His doctors were planning to testify against him, his car was bugged, his phone was tapped, his mail was being opened.[4]

At a restaurant on a road trip, Ernest decided two men standing together at the bar were FBI. When driving by a bank one evening, Ernest peered into the window, convinced the apparent cleaning people were really auditors going over his books.[5] Not only seeing this paranoia, Hotchner also saw Hemingway become depressed. He looked bad, he didn't want to go fishing or hunting, and he didn't invite people over to his house.

In the spring of 1961, Hemingway refused to go for more treatment at the Mayo Clinic. The doctors there wanted Ernest to come voluntarily, so Hotchner was called to try to broker a deal.

During one trip from Minnesota back to Ketchum, Ernest was traveling with four other people—his wife Mary, his nurse, friend Don Anderson, and friend Vernon Lord.

Once home, Ernest made a beeline for the front door ahead of the others. He slammed it closed and locked it. Don raced around to a side door and scrambled to the front of the house to find Ernest at the gun rack loading a shell into the chamber of his rifle. Don knocked Ernest to the floor before regaining control over the gun.[6]

The next day, Ernest agreed to return to the Mayo Clinic. Don and Vernon took him on a small plane under heavy sedation. The airplane, however, began to lose power and was forced to make an emergency landing in Casper, Wyoming.

As they left the plane, Ernest staggered toward the spinning propeller in a suicide attempt. Don grabbed him by the arm and risked his own life to get between Ernest and the lethal propeller. They later got Ernest back on the plane where he pretended to go to sleep. But as soon as the others left him alone, he leaped for the door, trying to jump out of the plane without a parachute.[7]

Once back at Mayo, a docile Ernest greeted the doctors like old friends. He answered all their questions correctly and enthusiastically. He was kept for treatment for the month. Mary was told not to come, since isolation was deemed part of the treatment. Electroshock continued and Hotchner said Ernest complained "his memory was wrecked and...he was ruined as a writer."[8]

Hotchner visited in June, driving up from Minneapolis. Ernest was stable and he asked permission from doctors for Hotchner to take him for a ride.

In the car, Ernest listed his woes, real and imagined. He said that there wouldn't be another spring, there wouldn't be another fall. Hotchner tried to steer the conversation to the future but Ernest wanted none of it.

Hotchner asked outright, "Why do you want to kill yourself?" Ernest answered forlornly, "Hotch, if I can't exist on my own terms, then existence is impossible. Do you understand? That is how I've lived, and that is how I must live—or not live."[9]

On June 14, 1961, Mary had dinner with Hotchner. Ernest was improving, the doctors said. He had shown interest in books, in hiking, and in abandoning his petty worries. They held out the idea of Ernest having a test-run of time at Ketchum. They estimated that he was 60 to 70 percent of his normal self. Hotchner was on his way to an assignment in Europe but another friend, George Brown, agreed to fly to Minnesota to drive Ernest and Mary back to Ketchum.

On Hemingway's first night home, they had a pleasant dinner and sang a favorite song before going to bed.[10]

Ernest took his life with a single shotgun blast that night. Mary jumped out of bed and ran to the first floor in the foyer of the Ketchum home. The blast killed Ernest instantly and blood was everywhere. Mary's first phone call was to Leonard Lyons, a Hollywood media columnist, with the instruction to tell people the gun went off accidentally while Ernest was cleaning it. Then she called for police and medical help.[11] Hotchner was in Spain. He telegraphed Mary with his condolences but could not make it in time for the funeral. Hotchner went to the Santa Maria Sopra Minerva Catholic Church—"his church, not mine"—to say goodbye to him.[12]

Mary Welsh Hemingway filed suit to block publication of Hotchner's biography *Papa Hemingway: A Personal Memoir,* arguing that it violated copyright. The story and the quotes were Ernest's, not Hotchner's.[13] Her suit delayed publication but did not prevent it.

Hotchner then filed a suit of his own over Jose Luis Castillo-Puche's *Hemingway in Spain* (Doubleday 1974) for libel and won a judgment in 1976. Hotchner convinced the court that the book contained fabricated and malicious descriptions of him and his relationship with Hemingway. The judge awarded $125,000 in damages and dismissed the publisher's appeal.

#2: Carlos Baker, *Ernest Hemingway: A Life Story*

Carlos Baker (1909-1987) was a professor at Princeton and was considered the foremost scholar of Ernest Hemingway's life. His initial publication, *Hemingway: The Writer as Artist* came out in 1952—nearly a decade before Hemingway's death. Immediately after his death, Baker revised the 1952 volume and reissued it in 1963. After all, Ernest had won the Nobel Prize (or "the Swedish thing" as he called it), so there was work to do. The final chapter of the re-issued volume speaks vaguely and sympathetically about Ernest's final days. The book strikes me as a functional chronology rather than a critical biography.

Baker immediately went to work on his critical masterpiece, *Ernest Hemingway: A Life Story* (MacMillan, 1969), in which he restated Ernest's story from beginning to end, in his typical fastidious scholarly manner—full of endnotes and references. The introduction to *A Life Story* is written beautifully. It captures so much meaning in its almost-poetic verse. Just reading the opening sentence of each paragraph is enough to taste the flavor (as it should be with good writing).

Still, even that volume abruptly ends with Ernest's suicide. There is no analysis of legacy, no consideration of the tensions that followed the death. Perhaps it was too fresh for a scholarly analysis, and he was the biographer who had worked with the approval of Ernest himself (and with this latter volume, his widow's). The Baker books (he edited a Letters volume years later) are the scholarly anchors of any understanding of Ernest's life and are generally cited in all works that have followed.

#3: Mary Welsh Hemingway, *How It Was*

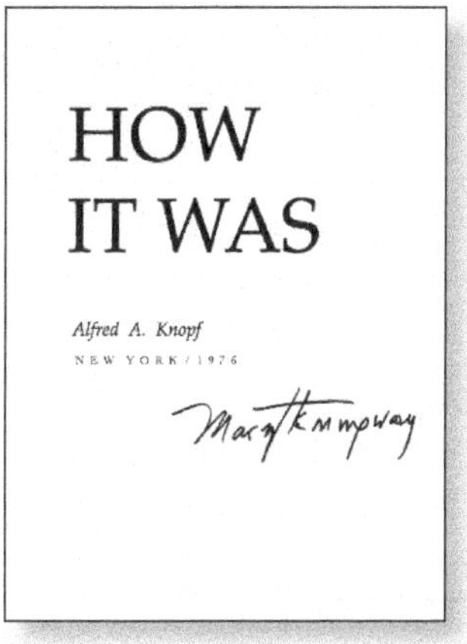

The third anchor biography came from Ernest's widow Mary Welsh Hemingway (1908-1986) in 1976—long after Baker and Hotchner. Her expansive memoir *How It Was* (Random House 1976) gave a brutally honest view of life with Ernest Hemingway in decline. She was married to Ernest longer than any other woman and lived with him in Cuba and Idaho. She had the job of managing his legacy after his death. She was an established writer when she married Ernest and oversaw the posthumous publication of multiple Hemingway works.

In Ernest's last decade, he had talked of a great trilogy of battle: air, land, and sea. The latter volume was the only one that materialized in any form, and it was not the battle-themed book he intended. Rather, it paralleled his own experiences in Bimini in 1936. Mary published it posthumously as *Islands in the Stream* in 1970.

The best posthumous piece, though, was 1964's *A Moveable Feast*—the telling memoir that Ernest was working on at the time of his death. Hotchner helped Mary edit the unfinished manuscript.

Biographies from His Family

Three of Hemingway's siblings published books about their brother. The first was from Marcelline Hemingway Sanford, *At the Hemingways: A Family Portrait* (Little Brown 1962). It already was in process at the time of Ernest's suicide in 1961, but she declared

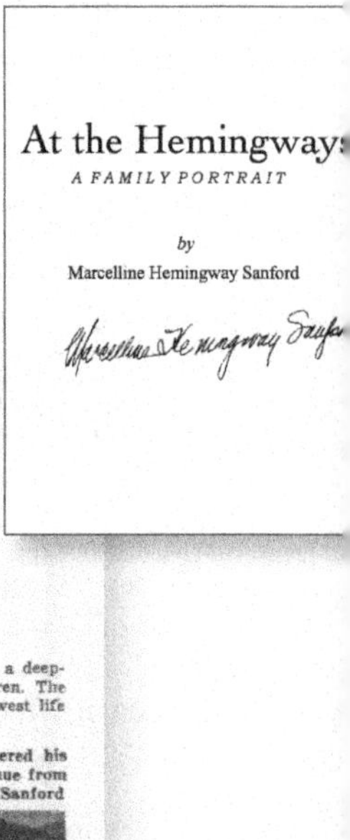

HER BOOK IS DUE AUG. 14

Ernest Hemingway's Sister Sets the Record Straight

By Jeanne Duran
Free Press Special Writer

MARCELLINE Hemingway Sanford glanced at the book in her hands. Titled "At the Hemingways," it bears her name as author. It is a warm and intimate account of her parents, her brothers and sisters, and especially of her brother Ernest.

"It is also a true account," says Mrs. Sanford, who finds the current movie, "Adventures of a Young Man," (billed as the Hemingway story) "fantastic," "offensive," even "laughable."

"The publishers had urged me for a long time to do the book, because Ernest and I were very close as children. There was only 18 months difference in our ages, but I was reluctant. He was an international figure, but it was hard for me to think of him in any way except as part of the family."

"However, I began to feel almost a moral obligation to present a real picture of all of us," she said.

Her book was in the hands of the printers last fall, when Ernest Hemingway died. It will be released by the publishers, Little, Brown and Company, Aug. 14, and has been chosen as the summer selection for the Young Adults Division of the Literary Guild.

Even Ernest himself twisted his own and the family's image, his sister says. "The current movie is based on several of his stories, including two he did

The result is a heartwarming book about a deep-rooted American couple and their six children. The reader gets a clear and detailed view of midwest life in the first quarter of our century.

"In winter Mr. Orth, our milkman, delivered his daily quarts to our house on Kenilworth Avenue from a square, low, open wooden bobsled," Mrs. Sanford writes, "and we children took delight in getting 'hitches' behind him on our small sleds or taking 'flops' behind other sleighs or the faster wagons on runners, the ones that delivered groceries . . . sometimes as many as six sleds clung by ropes . . . to the back of a horse-drawn wagon."

In another place the author tells of the "floor registers"—heat coming from the furnace through grillework in the floor, instead of wall outlets or radiators.

"Those big floor registers were wonderful things! The comfort of standing over

Mrs. Sanford

Newspapers.com; public domain

Detroit Free Press feature on sister ***Marcelline's*** *memoirs, which was really a response to Hotchner's screenplay of the Nick Adams stories—that were known to be adaptations (not portrayals) of Hemingway's life. Revealing biographies would not be released until Hotchner's 1966 work.*

that she would "set the record straight" after the film premier of Hemingway's *Adventures of a Young Man* (Twentieth Century Fox 1962). Filming had started just months after Hemingway's death and Hotchner wrote the screenplay. The movie deal had been arranged while Hemingway was still alive and it adapted some of his semi-biographical Nick Adams stories for the screen.

Other memoirs were published by the family. Sister Madelaine "Sunny" Miller wrote *Ernie: Hemingway's Sister "Sunny" Remembers* (Crown 1975), brother Leicester (pronounced "Lester"; he committed suicide in 1982) wrote *My Brother: Ernest Hemingway* (Winchester House 1962), son Jack Hemingway wrote *Misadventures of a Fly Fisherman: My Life with and without Papa* (McGraw Hill 1986), and son Gregory Hemingway wrote *Papa: A Personal Memoir* (Houghton Mifflin 1976). These are sentimental approaches that are filled with family life and lore. They add value to Ernest's story and reveal certain slivers of his background that may be less apparent or undeveloped in the work of others.

Son Patrick Hemingway (who has shied away from publicity) edited his father's *True at First Light: A Fictional*

ERNIE

Hemingway's *Sister "Sunny" Remembers*

by Madelaine Hemingway Miller

LEICESTER HEMINGWAY

My Brother,
Ernest Hemingway

JACK HEMINGWAY

MISADVENTURES OF A FLY FISHERMAN

My Life With and Without Papa

Papa

A Personal Memoir

Gregory H. Hemingway, M.D.

TRUE AT FIRST LIGHT

Edited with an Introduction by Patrick Hemingway

Memoir (Scribner 1999) and wrote introductions for other Hemingway works. Patrick, at the time of this writing, is still living in Montana at age 91. Subsequent generations have written numerous Hemingway-related tomes and, to be honest, I have not kept up with them nor have I considered them for this work. That is not a criticism of their worth or quality, but simply a line that had to be drawn for expediency's sake.

Biographies by and about His Wives

There are several volumes on the various Mrs. Hemingways.

Hadley Richardson Hemingway Mowrer was the first subject with Alice Sokoloff's *Hadley: The First Mrs. Hemingway* (Dodd Mead, 1973) and more recently the historical-fiction story in Paula McLain's *The Paris Wife* (Random House, 2014). The Sokoloff book was important because Hadley was the author's friend and informed its writing.

Gioia Diliberto produced the significant biography *Hadley* (Ticknor and Fields, 1992) and re-issued the book in a deeper form as *Paris without End* (Harper Perennial, 2011). Both are well-researched and build substantively on Sokoloff's work. Diliberto had the help of Hadley's sister's family, the Ushers, in writing the work. Both volumes have family photos not published elsewhere. A. E. Hotchner released *Hemingway in Love: His Own Story* (St. Martins, 2015) that added new detail to already-established stories of Hadley.

Pauline Pfeiffer's marriage to Ernest is the focus of Ruth Hawkins's study *Unbelievable Happiness and Final Sorrow* (University of Arkansas Press, 2012). This a thoughtful analysis published with the blessing of the Ernest Hemingway Foundation. It is a detailed account of Pauline's married years, but also the years that followed—with an intriguing Afterword. That last section has some of the most poignant information about how estates were settled, about decision-making for selling-off properties and about the human side of "after."

Martha Gellhorn wrote *Travels with Myself and Another: A Memoir* (Putnam 1978) that included a lot of detail about her few years with Hemingway—especially their trip to China. She has been the subject of a few thoughtful works. Professor Carl Rollyson wrote *Nothing Ever Happens to the Brave* (St. Martin's, 1990), a well-researched volume on Martha's life that finishes with an outstanding chronology of her life's work.

Martha was still living at the time of that publication. He updated the book after her death and reissued it a decade later as *Beautiful Exile* (Aurum Press, 2001). British author Caroline Moorehead's *Martha Gellhorn: A Life* (Random House, 2011) is rich in detail and well written. Martha had such a rich life before and after Hemingway that those wanting just a Hemingway-fix from her biography may be disappointed.

Bernice Galansky Kert (1923-2005), a St. Louis-born author who was a teaching fellow at the University of Michigan, produced *The Hemingway Women* (Norton, 1983). Kert did not start researching nonfiction work until age 50. Her nonfiction worked focused on women who lived in the shadows of great men (e.g., Hemingway and Rockefeller). This book is unique for the depth of its coverage of Mary Welsh Hemingway (albeit just a few chapters of section five). No biographer has tackled the fourth Mrs. Hemingway. Perhaps Mary's tell-all autobiography in 1976 has spoiled herself as a subject for other biographers.

The Narrowly-Focused Biographies

There have been many interesting volumes written about narrow chunks of Hemingway's life, either by people who knew him (e.g., Gregorio Fuentes, Arnold Samuelson, William Seward) or the places he went (e.g. *Hemingway in Michigan*, *Hemingway in Idaho*, *Hemingway's Key West*—and now *Hemingway's St. Louis*). These all have merit and contribute to our knowledge of the man and his work. Monty Python's Michael Palin, a Hemingway aficionado, wrote *Michael Palin's Hemingway Adventure* (St. Martins, 2001) and it is just plain fun as he tracks down people and places associated with Papa.

Charles Fenton's *Apprenticeship of Ernest Hemingway* (Farrar, Strauss & Young, 1954) is a richly-informed work for which he interviewed Y. K. Smith, Bill Smith, Carl Edgar, Ted Brumback, Bill Horne, Carlos Baker, Don Wright, and many others who were still accessible at that time. Though the questions are narrow, they are answered by those to whom Hemingway scholars would love to have access today. Thank goodness someone thought to talk to them!

Special mention goes to the Arnold Samuelson work, *With Hemingway* (Holt Rinehart & Winston, 1984). Samuelson was a 22-year-old budding writer when he showed up in Key West hoping for a few minutes of the author's time. He spent, instead, the next year of his life working on Hemingway's boat and meeting his friends.

Samuelson was quite intelligent, was musically inclined, and wrote profusely. Paul Hendrickson, in his 2011 biography of Hemingway, describes Samuelson as an emotionally-tortured man.[14] He was married with two children, and divorced when his behavior became too violent. He lived an eccentric life and people just thought he was crazy. He roamed his property naked. He collected, and played, old fiddles. He had a white beard that rivaled Ernest's. When he went out, he dressed as if he were a rag-picker's son. He fashioned his sandals out of old tires, he drove around with his horse in the back of a beat-up truck, and he had the occasional run-in with the law. He lost all his hair and all his teeth. The photo on his driver's license, described Hendrickson, was "almost scary."[15] But overall his actions were, as Hendrickson put it, harmless actings-out of the town crank.[16] He was found dead in 1981, sprawled out naked on the ground, having just returned from the grocery store—a heart attack at age 69. As his family cleaned out his years of strange accumulations, the manuscript of his year with Hemingway was uncovered and published posthumously.

The Substantial Biographies

There are several authors worthy of special praise for their work documenting Ernest Hemingway's life. Excellent biographies of Hemingway appeared in the 1980s and 1990s—Peter Griffin wrote a very strong series, as has Michael Reynolds and Scott Donaldson—all top-notch authors.

Peter Griffin wrote *Along with Youth* (Oxford, 1985), which covered Hemingway's boyhood years, and *Less Than a Treason* (Oxford, 1990), which covered the Paris years. He received his doctorate from Brown University and taught at MIT. Sadly, Griffin died at age 59 in 2002 before he could complete the series.

Michael Reynolds wrote a series of five Hemingway biographies, all excellent sources on the author's life. He died in 2000 at age 63, but he lived long enough to chronicle Hemingway's life from *The Young Hemingway* (Blackwell, 1986) to *Hemingway: The Final Years* (Norton, 1999). They are reliable, well-researched books, and fill the gap left by Griffin's unfinished work.

Scott Donaldson is the most prolific Hemingway biographer. His work is strong and dependable, and Hemingway scholars owe a debt of gratitude to him. Donaldson published his first Hemingway volume *By Force of Will* (Viking Press, 1977) ahead of most other studies, and has written extensively on Hemingway and others in the "Paris in the 20's" circle. He is retired from the College of William and Mary and still publishes, most recently *The Paris Husband* (Charly, 2018), a witty nonfiction response to the novel *The Paris Wife.*

Kenneth S. Lynn (1923-2001) produced a major volume *Hemingway* (Simon and Schuster, 1987). Lynn was a history professor at Johns Hopkins. It is a solid piece of academic work and makes a strong general reference for any Hemingway student.

Freelance writer James Mellow produced *Hemingway: A Life without Consequences* (Houghton Mifflin 1992). The original volume is profusely illustrated and is a pleasure to read. He died in 1997.

University of Colorado Professor Jeffrey Meyers (born 1939) wrote *Hemingway: A Biography* (Harper and Row, 1985). Meyers' work has informed Rollyson's biographies of Martha Gellhorn and speaks to his insight on that subject.

Paul Hendrickson's well-researched and well-written volume *Hemingway's Boat: Everything He Loved in Life, and Lost, 1934-1961* (Knopf 2011), was my favorite among the biographies of the last decade. Hendrickson (born 1944) is a senior lecturer at the University of Pennsylvania and an alumnus of St. Louis University.

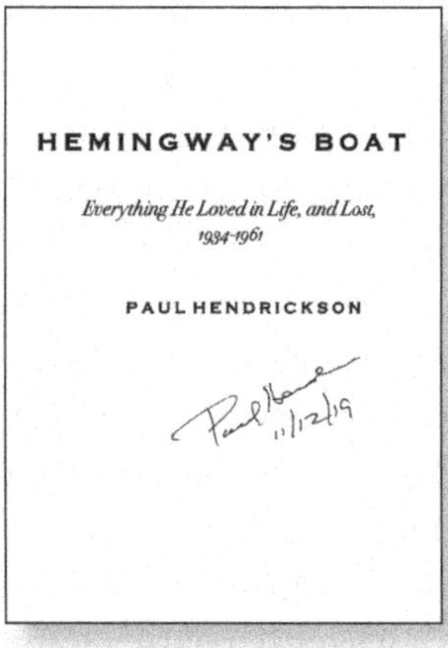

He chronicled Ernest's life through the pursuit of the *Pilar* and the role it played in his adventures thereafter. These were stories about Hemingway that are told nowhere else. His "Essay on Sources" was so thoughtful that it inspired me to add this commentary on what I found useful. It was my pleasure to get to meet him on a "hometown" visit in 2019. It was a great joy in my life to travel to Cuba in 2013 as part of an exchange program my university had with the University of Havana. I got to see Hemingway's boat, *Pilar*. It was both happy and sad.

Biographies that are quite good and worth a look include Brian's collection of interviews in *The True Gen* (Delta 1988), Villard and Nagel's *Hemingway in Love and War* (Northeastern University Press 1989), and Lyttle's *Ernest Hemingway* (Atheneum, 1992). James Nagel has written multiple books on Hemingway, all good volumes. Brian's book gets the gold star for the best cover photo—a colorized image of Hemingway reclined seemingly naked on his bed, reading *The New York Times* with his "black dog" curled up alongside.

I have only recently finished Mary Dearborn's *Ernest Hemingway: A Biography* (Knopf 2017) and appreciated the way she unpacks personality in her analyses of various situations. It is clear that she does deep research and is well-informed. It is a substantial biography. The illustrations in this book are brilliant choices—beyond the usual ones found in other biographies.

How Life Unrolled

I have mentioned many titles here, and briefly reviewed only a few. It represents only a sliver of my Hemingway library and there are so many more volumes that are not (yet) in my collection. Their presence or absence does not speak to their quality or utility, and my take on a volume is purely personal academic taste—I respect that these are all worthy books (hey—I paid good money for each of them!) and that some were more useful for my purposes than others.

All of these works, including this monograph, are celebrating Ernest Hemingway, a perfectly imperfect man. Despite his demons, he advanced American literature—nay, *world literature* according to the Nobel Prize committee. He sought adventure and he found it. He linked life with literature. His novels capture some readers, others are captured by his biography. All of us acknowledge that something impressive happened. Bill Smith said in an interview that Hemingway's genius "would have made it whatever way his life had unrolled."[17]

Yet, his life unrolled in a very specific way, and that way all started because of a few St. Louisans who went north for the summers.

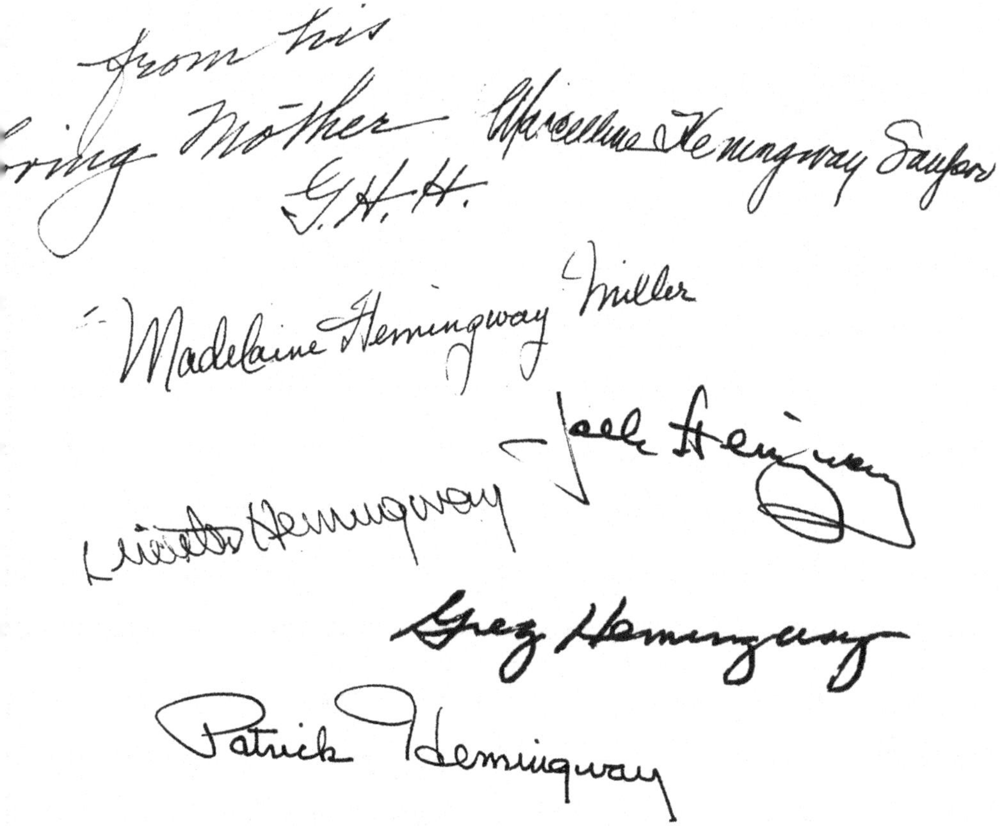

Untimely Ends

Smith family	LIFESPAN	CAUSE OF DEATH, AGE
Kate Merrill Smith (Katy's mother)	1863-1899	Tuberculosis at 36
Merrill Smith (Katy's brother)	1883-1924	Burst appendix at 40
Wanda Stopa (Y.K. Smith's lover)	1900-1924	Suicide at 23
Katy Smith herself	1891-1947	Car crash at 55

Richardson family		
James Richardson (Hadley's father)	1855-1905	Suicide at 50
Helen Breaker (Hadley's friend)	1890-1936	Suicide at 46

Pfeiffer family		
Pauline Pfeiffer	1895-1951	Died in surgery at 56

Gellhorn family		
Martha Gellhorn	1908-1998	Suicide at 89

Hemingway family		
Clarence Hemingway (Ernest's father)	1871-1928	Suicide at 57
Ernest himself	**1899-1961**	**Suicide at 61**
Ursula Hemingway (sister)	1902-1966	Suicide at 64
Leicester Hemingway (brother)	1915-1982	Suicide at 67
Margaux Hemingway (granddaughter)	1954-1996	Drug overdose at 42
Gregory Hemingway (son)	1931-2001	Cardiac event in jail at 69

Endnotes

Introduction

1. See Baker 1969, pp. 30, 60

Chapter 1 – The Smith Family

1. Browne 37. This birthdate was difficult to find and verify. She lied about her age on her marriage license, which misinformed her tombstone, and she lied in the 1920 census. Also, she attributes her birthplace to Louisiana in the census (which makes finding source documents like census and birth certificates futile), but I knew her father was not working at Tulane at that time. Her birthdate and birthplace surfaced in a biography of her father from 1961. This confirms Rintoul on the date and my general suspicions on the birthplace. Like her brother Bill, she probably was born across the river in East St. Louis, Illinois, rather than St. Louis, Missouri.
2. Diliberto 1992, 50
3. Intense fans of the series Mad Men will remember the last few minutes of Season 1 Episode 4 (New Amsterdam) when the character Trudy Campbell is extolling how her husband Pete Campbell is descended from the Dyckman family. Yes, this stuff really does touch real lives!
4. Allow me to say that, as a scholar, I have made my life's work the study of East St. Louis's industrial legacy and encourage you to find my book Made in USA (Virginia Publishing, 2003) or the public television documentary of the same name to learn more about this little city and the effects industry had upon it. The St. Louis Public Library can assist.

5. "East St. Louis: Death of Ex-Postmaster Gilbert B. Foster," St. Louis Post-Dispatch. 20 Jul 1894.

6. The National Hotel was heavily damaged by a gigantic tornado in May of 1896 that roared through St. Louis and East St. Louis; this probably precipitated Laura's move across the river to St. Louis by the time the 1898 city directory was compiled.

7. See, for example, "A Fine Ranch Property," Los Angeles Times. 05 Jan 1902. Pg. 11.

8. Browne 301. Warren Browne, who wrote the authoritative biography of William Benjamin Smith, says that everyone (including Dr. Smith) said that Kate's formal name was Kathleen. Her death record reads this way. However, Browne says that a relative insisted that her name was Katharine and produced the family Bible to prove it. This would explain why the first daughter is named Katharine. Browne's work uses the biblical name; this book uses the name of record.

9. See "Weddings Elsewhere," The Sedalia Weekly Bazoo. 07 Nov 1882. Pg. 5.

10. Browne 60

11. "Society," St. Louis Post-Dispatch. 03 Jul 1892. Filmstrip pg. 10.

12. Severance 8

13. Opera: Severance 14; Church: Browne 37; best music: Swisher 42.

14. Browne 37

15. See the society column, St. Louis Post-Dispatch. 02 Aug 1896. Pg. 24.

16. See "Society Notes," The Times-Democrat, New Orleans LA. 15 Jul 1894. Pg. 1, 3rd column.

17. According to Bill Smith's World War II "Old Man" draft card, he claimed his birthplace was East St. Louis, Illinois. The only logical reason Kate would have given birth there was to be in the company of her widowed sister who was still living in the National Hotel. See Registration Card (Men born on or after April 28, 1877 and on or before February 16, 1897), Serial Number #U3143 for William B. Smith, born 20 Aug 1895 at E. St. Louis, Illinois; entered by registrar Emma McCarthy, Local Board 19, NY, NY. The date stamp is missing and replaced with a handwritten number. The form revision date was 01 Apr 1942, which gives the earliest possible date.

18. Kathleen's death notice is found in "Local News," Charlevoix Sentinel. 14 Jun 1899. Col. 2, pg. 1.

19. "Pre-Prohibition Sentiment Drives Away Brew King's Family,"

Petoskey News. Posted: 27 Nov 2015. Accessed: 24 Aug 2019. https://www.petoskeynews.com/ charlevoix/news/community/pre-prohibition-sentiment-drives-away-brew-king-s- family/article_4cc38f97-75d4-5421-9a03-5a9ace29a8f2.html

20. Frantz's book The Belvedere Club places Kathleen Merrill Smith at the Belvedere Hotel as early as 1887 (online version is not paginated; see page 15 of the PDF version).

21. Some sources suggest that Katy lived with her widowed father and two brothers, but it is not supported by the father's entry in the 1900 census or the Browne biography. Browne's genealogy (taken from the family Bible) gives Merrill's birthdate as 23 Aug 1883 and Kenley's as 05 Dec 1885 (pp. 329-330). There is confusion about Kenley's birth year just as there is with Katy's. The work accepts the family Bible data in Browne as the best available.

22. For the train passenger list, see "Petoskey, Michigan," St. Louis Republic. 14 Jul 1901. Pg. 9.

23. Dr. Joseph Charles, over the years 1945-1947, wrote an autobiographical manuscript that is in the collection of the Missouri History Museum in St. Louis. He notes (incorrectly) that he married Laura Foster in 1901 (rather, they MET in 1901) and notes that Laura's mother lived with her and the niece and nephew. See Joseph William Charles. Eight[y] Years of Ordinary Life: or from Country Practitioner to City Specialist, manuscript, Missouri Historical Society Archives, St. Louis. Pg. 53.

24. See "Charles-Foster Nuptials," St. Louis Republic. 22 May 1902.

25. Laura M. Charles bought Cottage #513 from the widow of Civil War General John H. King in 1903 and sold the property to Gertrude P. Brown in 1916 (Frantz PDF page 147). Diliberto gives the purchase year of the Stroud property as 1902, probably informed by the marriage of Aunty Laura to Dr. Joseph. Carlos Baker (1969) gives the date as 1912, probably informed by the death date of Alonzo Stroud. Baker's research is outstanding, and likely he is correct. The 1910 Census for this township starts with Alonzo Stroud and his wife, but there is no street address. However, just a few entries "down the street" on the census form is the Dilworth family, who would have been physically located very close to what became Charles Farm.

26. Griffin 35. Griffin gives a nice description of the land.

27. Baker 1969, 25

28. Fenton 28

29. Dearborn 42-44. The "summer people" appear to have started hanging around together in 1916 and all documented associations are

after that point. Katy Smith vouched for Ernest in his 1923 passport renewal, according to NARA records. She claimed she had known Ernest for 7 years as of November 23, 1921—implying they met in or around 1914, certainly possible but a bit earlier than the accepted year. (There are multiple examples of Katy lying about dates on official forms; if "7 years" was important for this passport task, then she would have stretched the truth readily.)

30. Baker 1969, 25

31. Baker 1969, 25

32. Carr 258

33. Carr 282

34. Carr 257. Sherwood Anderson writes in "A Midwestern Ad Man Remembers," Advertising and Selling (25 Mar 1937, p. 58) that Katy was a regular contributor to Woman's Home Companion and for a brief time in Chicago was the "Advertising Manager" for the Eskimo Pie brand. Eskimo Pie was patented in 1922 and Katie left Chicago before 1925, so the opportunity must have been brief. Charles Duan notes in Slate's "Ice Cream Headache," (20 Oct 2015) that one million Eskimo Pies were being sold each day in 1922. Duan also notes that the partnership that formed it in 1922 (Iowa dairyman Christian Nelson and Chicago chocolatier Russell Stover) sold out in 1923—perhaps also ending Katy's Chicago-based management of the product.

35. Carr 256

36. Carr 258, 456

37. St. John 166

38. St. John 167

39. Diliberto 1992 85

40. Mellow 160

41. Griffin 35; you can see a brass-trimmed Ford touring car on Clive Baugh's excellent Hemingway travel blog page: http://clive-w.blogspot.com.

42. Severance 5

43. Severance 8

44. See, generally, the Severance and Browne biographies for these details and more.

45. The Wikipedia entry for Dr. Smith is surprisingly accurate: "William Benjamin Smith," Wikipedia: The Free Encyclopedia. https://en.wikipedia.org/wiki/William_Benjamin_Smith; posted: n.d.;

accessed: 24 Aug 2019. You can also read his abhorrent book The Color Line: A Brief in Behalf of the Unborn. (McClure, 1905).

46. It ran in many papers. See, for example, "Negro Race to be Extinct in 2123," Victoria, Texas, Daily Advocate. 11 Dec 1912. Pg 1.

47. St. John 166-167; Mellow 37

48. Browne 61

49. Mellow 37 Since Y.K. lived with Professor Smith, it would make sense that the Professor would be in Horton Bay during Y.K.'s visit.

50. Severance 9

51. Severance 14

52. Severance 14

53. "Dr. W. B. Smith, 83, Philosopher, Dead," The New York Times. 07 Aug 1934. The Findagrave entry has been updated as part of this research: https://www.findagrave.com/memorial/96888395/william-benjamin-smith.

54. Browne 250-251. Apparently, the estate included some acreage in Arkansas that Bill tried to farm for a time, but gave up; see Carr 256.

55. St. John 177

56. "WeeJun" is found in Frantz PDF 22, "Wemedge" is found in Hemingway's short story about he and Bill, "The Three-Day Blow." There were many in Ernest's life who used nicknames, including his parents, but for Ernest it was Bill Smith's use of them that seemed to have some staying power.

57. Gould's 1920 and 1921 directories under "Smith, Wm. B. Jr."

58. Home sale from Miller to Charles: see "Westminster Place Home Sold," St. Louis Post-Dispatch. 31 Oct 1920. Patsy Ruth Miller is easily found online.

59. Gould's 1920 directory under "Charles, Benj H." 890.

60. Blume 232; they were married in New Jersey in 1939 (see New Jersey Marriage Index for that year).

61. Blume 129

62. Blume 129

63. Rintoul 842

64. There are multiple references to this, but this point is well-illustrated by Carr, pg. 258.

65. Baker 1969, 49

66. According to Johnston (pg. 272), "The Three-Day Blow" is based on real-life events that can be traced to Horton Bay—and he traces most all of them. One must conclude that the drinking was a real-life event too.

67. Carr 258, among other examples.

68. See Malvine Cole's letter to the New York Times 20 July 1986, Section 6, page 62, with the headline "The Hemingway Letters."

69. It is on the eBay site: https://www.ebay.com/itm/FOR-WHOM-THE-BELL-TOLLS-SIGNED-BY-ERNEST-HEMINGWAY-USING-HIS-YOUTH-NICKNAME/382961314242?hash=item592a45e9c2:g:DiQAAOSwkXRbZd2Y; posted in August 2019 and still active in January 2020. The initial asking price was $12,000.

70. Browne 37; the parents' names were Jeremiah H. "Jerry" Smith (1814-1864) and Angelina Kenley (1816-1892)

71. Griffin 120. The statement is unsourced. However, it makes sense especially since Y.K. and his sister Katy seem connected thereafter. There are no entries for Y.K. or Bill Smith in the Gould St. Louis city directories for 1917-18 or 1916-17. His WWI draft registration card from June 5, 1917, gives his home address as 608 South Cloud, Syracuse NY (Card 26721, No. 43 found on Fold3.com under "Geremya Kenley Smith").

72. Mellow 127; Sherwood Anderson writes in "A Midwestern Ad Man Remembers," Advertising and Selling (28 Jan 1937, p. 66) that Y. K. Smith had a newspaper column called "Glot's Slots" in a Syracuse newspaper briefly before coming to Critchfield's in Chicago. It could have been something to pay the bills while confined to the sanatorium.

73. Dearborn 95. His employer is a minor point, but there is a lot said about it. Liesl Olson's Chicago Renaissance (Yale, 2017) says it was actually "Taylor-Critchfield" at the time and that Sherwood Anderson worked there too (pg. 161). The 07 Aug 1920 edition of Advertising and Selling (pg. 41) notes in "New Copy Director for Grieg & Ward" that Y.K. left his copywriting/account executive post with "Critchfield & Co." to be the director of copy for "Grieg & Ward." Further, the blurb states that Y.K. had been associate editor of Farm Mechanics and American Builder. Mellow (pg. 127) suggests that he worked for McCann Erickson, but the source is unclear. He may have thought this because Y.K. worked on the Coca Cola account (which McCann held at various points in time). The most likely employer for Y.K. in his Manhattan years was D'Arcy (Diliberto 1992, 45)—an esteemed St. Louis firm that won the Coca Cola account and created the "Santa Claus" ads that helped shift Coke from a summertime drink to year-round. (See Ad Age feature,

"D'Arcy Advertising Co.," AdAge Encyclopedia. Posted: 15 Sep 2003. Accessed: 24 Aug 2019. https://adage.com/article/adage-encyclopedia/d-arcy-advertising/98612.)].

74. Baker 1969, 78. Apparently Y.K. had multiple large apartments in Chicago over the early 1920s, and some Hemingway biographies refer to different addresses. The 1920 Census places him in a large property in Oak Park January of that year. I consider Baker to be the definitive source. The apartment called the "Domicile," where Hadley met Ernest in the fall of 1920, was at this address on Division. Confirmed by Olson's Chicago Renaissance (161) and Dearborn (98).

75. Reynolds 1986, 207

76. "Good Girl Gone Bad," Chicago Tribune.

77. "Good Girl Gone Bad," Chicago Tribune.

78. "Good Girl Gone Bad" and "Wandering Wanda," Chicago Tribune.

79. The photos of the crowd are quite amazing and are posted on the Tribune's website: http://galleries.apps.chicagotribune.com/chi-130409-wanda-stopa-pictures/

80. Reynolds 1986, 207

81. St. John 155, 157-8

82. Baker 1969, 88

83. See Browne 301, who says Y.K. in 1961 was living with his third wife (unnamed) on a farm on Cockertown Road in Red Hook, NY. She is identified in Ken Culbertson's 1998 Nobody Said Not to Go: The Life, Loves, and Adventures of Emily Hahn. Open Road edition. New York: Open Road Media, 2016. The Google books version is not paginated, but the reference is searchable.

84. St. John 166

85. Cappell (Montgomery) 185

86. The Griffin biography raises this point about Dr. Charles being only an "optometrist" who insisted on being called "doctor" (suggesting that an optometrist is not a real doctor), and that Ernest resented this. (Griffin 172) Ernest grossly underestimated Dr. Charles's professional worth.

87. "Dr. Joseph W. Charles, Eye Specialist," St. Louis Post-Dispatch. 10 Feb 1950.

88. His manuscript is only about his professional work. See Charles, Joseph William. Eight[y] Years of Ordinary Life: or from Country Practitioner to City Specialist, manuscript, Missouri Historical

Society Archives, St. Louis. Pg. 53.

89. See "11 Typhoid Deaths Here Since April 1," St. Louis Post-Dispatch 03 Aug 1924, Pg. 8B. Also, "Atrocities of our Deadliest Enemy—The Fly," Springfield News-Leader, 04 May 1924, Pg. 23.

90. See "Ernest Hemingway," Charlevoix. https://www.visitcharlevoix.com/ Ernest_Hemingway_. Posted: N.D. Accessed: 24 Aug 2019.

91. Baker 1969, 77

92. The nickname for the bachelor pad, Baker 1969, 78

93. Baker 1969, 76

94. Baker 1969, 78

95. Baker 1969, 77

96. Baker 1969, 77

97. Browne 241

98. Carr 260

99. Carr 258-261. Edith Foley married Frank Shay, Bill Smith married Marion Hammett, and all of them overlapped with Katy and Dos at Smooley Hall over the years. See references to these overlaps by Carr, Dearborn, and Marion Hammett Smith. Arequipa house is a bit of a Cape Cod landmark now: see "571 Commercial Street," Building Provincetown. <https://buildingprovincetown.wordpress.com/2010/01/07/571-commercial-street/>. Posted: 01 Jan 2010. Accessed: 24 Aug 2019.

Chapter 2 - The Richardson Family

1. Baker 1969 78

2. Cappell (Montgomery) 198

3. Griffin 159

4. Diliberto 1992, 49

5. Griffin 160

6. Griffin 160

7. See, for example, Gould's 1919 directory for Usher (pg. 2341) and Richardson (pg. 1951). Diliberto (1992) describes the shared entrance on page 26.

8. Diliberto 1992, 57

9. Diliberto 1992, 57; Bertha L. Doane (1878-1960) was a librarian at the St. Louis Cabanne Branch Library. Her last name is often misspelled.
10. Diliberto 1992, 68; Ruth Bradfield (1891-1976) married Dr. Lee Pettit Gay (1894-1960) in an impromptu wedding in 1923; George and Helen Breaker were the only guests. Ruth sued for divorce in 1940, having been separated for a year. Lee married again in 1941 and divorced again in 1942.
11. Griffin 182. Though not mentioned by name, the restaurant described could only be the fashionable Busch's Grove. The restaurant is gone today, but its distinctive fried potatoes are still available at the Union30 Restaurant inside the Hotel St. Louis.
12. For the record, the Griffin text has a minor error "Litzminger" Road should be "Litzsinger" Road. Griffin 182, 247
13. Griffin 181; Diliberto 1992, 69
14. Griffin 173
15. Diliberto 1992, 69
16. Baker 1969, 79
17. Diliberto 1992, 70
18. Griffin 183
19. Diliberto 1992, 71
20. Gould's 1921, 705
21. Diliberto 1992, 72
22. Diliberto 1992, 78-80
23. Diliberto 1992, 78-80
24. Sokoloff 35
25. Diliberto 1992, 80-81
26. Notable alums include artist Thomas Hart Benton (who did not complete his studies) and St. Louisan Edward "Butch" O'Hare, for whom Chicago's O'Hare Airport is named.
27. Diliberto 1992, 2-3; inflation adjusted using the westegg.com/inflation calculator. The drug company also dealt in tobacco and cigars: see "L. D. Cabanne in Omaha," St. Louis Post-Dispatch, 20 Apr 1890, p. 16.
28. Diliberto 1992, 3
29. Diliberto 1992, 3 (preceding sentence also)
30. Diliberto 1992, 4

31. See "Revolt of Wives," The New Republic, 05 Jun 1915. Pp. 122-123.

32. Diliberto 1992, 4; "Revolt of Wives," 122-123.

33. Diliberto 1992, 5; she accomplished this by feeding Holofernes salty starchy pancakes that made him thirst and consume too much wine—hence the latke tradition in Judaism, said Jayne Cohen to CBS News. See "Behind the Hanukkah Tradition of Latkes," CBS Sunday Morning. 22 Dec 2019.

34. Diliberto 1992, 3

35. Diliberto 1992, 6

36. See "Wife of Orrick Johns, Author, Dies in West," St. Louis Republic. 16 Jul 1936. Pg. 5.

37. Diliberto 1992, 18

38. Diliberto 1992, 17-18

39. Diliberto 1992, 4

40. See "Financial Worry Cause of Suicide," St. Louis Globe-Democrat. 09 Feb 1905, microfilm page 14.

41. Diliberto 1992, 12

42. Diliberto 1992, 13

43. The addition probably added kitchen and plumbing to the second floor so that it could function as an apartment independent of the first floor. Florence occupied the second floor with Hadley, and the Usher Family occupied the first floor. This addition probably coincided with Fonnie's marriage in 1910. Diliberto notes that Hadley moved in with her mother after leaving Bryn Mawr in 1912, which supports the idea that the addition was motivated by the establishment of the Usher household on the first floor. Diliberto 1992, 26

44. Diliberto 1992, 18

45. Diliberto 1992, 19

46. Diliberto 1992, 19

47. Griffin 160. On this page, an "R" is accidentally added to the child's name. The child grew up to be an accomplished artist, Fonchen Lord, about whom much is readily found.

48. Diliberto 1992, 30-31

49. Diliberto 1992, 60

50. Diliberto 1992, 60

51. Diliberto 1992, 59; Fonnie judged Ernest to be "selfish, unsympathetic, and very young." (Griffin 161)

52. Diliberto 1992, 70
53. Gould's 1920, 2702
54. It is unclear how many rooms were available to rent, or if there was more property to rent than just the duplex. Dilliberto 1992, 70
55. Hemingway used the foul term.
56. Diliberto 1992, 70-71—Diliberto prints the full text of the poem here.
57. Griffin 183-184; The Becker Library Archives at Washington University in St. Louis has several interesting pieces of Dr. Schwab's professional papers. I have not investigated if any of this pertains to the subjects of this book.
58. Diliberto 1992, 56-57
59. Diliberto 1992, 26 (hurling insults) and 71 (wheels)
60. Diliberto 1992, 71
61. Griffin 216. Griffin adds an interesting piece of information—Hadley had originally planned to arrive August 30. Page 216 has an obvious typo, giving the date as September 7 instead of 2.
62. Sokoloff 37; Diliberto 1992, 84-85
63. Griffin 216
64. Diliberto 1992, 85
65. Diliberto 1992, 85-86
66. Griffin 199
67. There is a lot of confusion about the wedding party. The Mellow biography says Helen Breaker was the Maid of Honor and Ursula Hemingway was an attendant (Mellow 140). The Sokoloff biography states that Bill Horne was best man (Sokoloff 39), as does the Dearborn biography (Dearborn 104). The Kenneth Lynn biography of Hemingway affirms Bill Smith as best man (Lynn 143). The Griffin biography said Ernest refused to select "a best man" among the two groomsmen (Griffin 217). Griffin may have based his understanding from the fictionalized account in Hemingway's "Wedding Day." Bill Smith himself, in his 1968 interview with Donald St. John, said he was to be the best man for Ernest at the desired wedding to Agnes von Kurowsky and wound up being best man at Ernest's wedding to Hadley (St. John 159). Bill Horne notes that he was an usher in a 1979 Princeton alumni interview. See "First Person: The Hemingway I Remember," Princeton Alumni Weekly. 11 Nov 1979. For purposes of this work, I'm going with the Smith and Horne interviews.
68. Cappell (Montgomery) 198

69. Baker 1969, 78, 82

70. The annual amount is agreed upon in sources (Baker, 1992, 78, 82). Most repeat the Baker information (e.g., Diliberto 1992, 176) but it seems that Baker got this info from Hadley herself. The grand total is surmised best by Reynolds 1989 (178-9); which Diliberto 1992 supports (177). This is different than the inherited amounts upon her father's death, but would include growth over time and additions from her mother's estate. Westegg.com/inflation was the inflation calculator used.

71. Told in many places, including "Ezra Pound's Kickstarter Plan for T. S. Eliot," Mentalfloss. Posted 08 Dec 2013. Accessed: 24 Aug 2019. http://mentalfloss.com/article/54098/ezra-pounds-kickstarter-plan-ts-eliot

72. Reynolds 1989, 178-179

73. Reynolds 1989, 179

74. Gould's 1921 705

75. A person functionally had to be "invited" to live on Kingsbury Place or its affluent neighbor Portland Place. Hadley's parents had received an invitation to build but turned it down to stay on still-desirable Cabanne Avenue, which was near Florence's brothers.

76. Gould's 1921, 2055

77. There is a minor misspelling of this name, "Allentown" rather than "Allenton," in some works (Diliberto 1992, 178; Griffin 145). This area is part of the City of Eureka today, and Allenton Road still runs along here by the Six Flags amusement park.

78. See "Inquiry into Bank Recalls Breaker Promotion Plans," St. Louis Star-Times, 17 Jan 1927, pg. 2.

79. See "Grand Jury Goes Into Failure of Two Banks," St. Louis Globe-Democrat. 20 Dec 1927. Pg. 18. See also "Charges Dropped Against Allenton Bank Officials," St. Louis Star. 23 Jul 1931, pg. 3.

80. Voss 24; divorce: "Mrs. Breaker Gets Divorce 48 Hours After Filing Suit," St. Louis Post-Dispatch. 17 Dec 1926, pg. 18.

81. Kennedy Library: One of Helen's portraits of Ernest graces the dust jacket of Peter Griffin's biography Less Than a Treason. Another is the cover for Nicholas Gerogiannis's Complete Poems. Revised ed. Lincoln: University of Nebraska Press, (1979) 1992. Suicide and note: See "Mrs. H. P. Breaker Ends Life in Paris by Inhaling Gas," St. Louis Star, 14 Dec 1936, p. 1; "60-Page Suicide Note Left by Mrs. Breaker," St. Louis Globe-Democrat, 15 Dec 1936, pg. 7A. Mother's death 13 Oct 1936: Lucie Alexander Pierce (1868-1936) Findagrave.com.

82. There are a few sources that accidentally mix up the Wyman brothers. Arthur (who died in 1935) is confused with Frank (who died in 1924) (Sokoloff 40; Diliberto 1992, 92). The Wyman Center of St. Louis today is named for Postmaster Frank Wyman.
83. Sokoloff 40
84. Baker 1969, 79
85. See the "Fragments" section of the 2009 "restored" edition. The Google books version is not paginated, but worth exploring. Bibliographic entry: Hemingway, Ernest. A Moveable Feast . Restored Edition/Scribner Classics. New York: Simon and Schuster, 2009. Ebook edition, 2014.
86. Koontz 41

Chapter 3 - The Pfeiffer Family

1. Entry #43 in Philosophical Writings and Aphorisms of Gustavus A. Pfeiffer. New York: Privately Printed, 1955. The book is not paginated.
2. Hawkins 43-44; Hawkins 50
3. Hawkins 54
4. Hawkins 46; Diliberto 1992, 205
5. Baker 1969, 173
6. Baker, 1969, 185
7. The Google Books version is not paginated, but worth exploring. See the Foreword by Patrick Hemingway, using the table of contents link. Bibliographic entry: Hemingway, Ernest. A Moveable Feast. Restored Edition/Scribner Classics. New York: Simon and Schuster, 2009. Ebook edition, 2014. In truth, Ernest probably had nothing to do with the title of the posthumous book.
8. Leland 97. There are many tellings of this story.
9. See Ellenberger, Allan R. "Sins of the Mother: The Story of Pauline Hemingway," Hollywoodland: A Site about Hollywood and Its History. Posted 02 Dec 2015. Accessed: 24 Aug 2019. http://allanellenberger.com/sins-of-the-mother-the-story-of-pauline-hemingway/comment-page-1/
10. Laymon 43
11. Laymon 43

12. Laymon 43-44
13. "Heavy Increase of Capital," St. Louis Globe-Democrat. 03 Jul 1901, pg. 7. The company called itself the Allan-Pfeiffer Manufacturing Company at first, specifying "manufacturing chemists" on its 1892 letterhead. It would become the Allan-Pfeiffer Chemical Company after the 1901 reorganization.
14. "At St. Louis...," The Palmyra Spectator, 31 Oct 1985, pg. 8.
15. "Will Build $40,000 Plant," St. Louis Globe-Democrat. 21 Jun 1913, pg. 7.
16. Back in the day, much of today's Delmar Boulevard was called Morgan Street. The name was changed in the 1930s. See the Gould directories for 1902 and 1906 (pg. 1356). For the children, see Lymon 70, 229.
17. Laymon 18, 50
18. Warner Pharmaceutical would merge in 1955 with a great St. Louis firm, the Lambert Pharmacal Company (inventors of Listerine mouthwash and family for whom the St. Louis airport is named), creating the powerful Warner-Lambert company that is now part of Pfizer (see, for example, Dearborn 205).
19. See "Timeline," The Hemingway-Pfeiffer Museum and Educational Center, January 1920. Posted: n.d.; Accessed: 13 Oct 2019. <https://hemingway.astate.edu/history/ timeline/> Conde Nast's mother was Esther Benoist, daughter of St. Louis banker Louis A. Benoist.
20. Hawkins 56-57
21. Baker 1969, 175
22. Baker 1969, 202-203
23. Baker 1969, 185
24. Hawkins 73
25. Hawkins 76
26. There is some confusion among the sources. Hawkins spells the street name "Feron" (pg. 70) but Dearborn has it "Ferou" (pg. 236). Dearborn states the rent as 9000 francs a year (source unclear) and Hawkins gives it as 900 francs per month (source identified). Dearborn's comparison to $30 per month does match my computation from historicalstatistics.org for 750 francs (1/12th of 9,000). I'm using the Dearborn spelling and Hawkins number with citation.
27. Hawkins 47

28. Hawkins 47
29. The trust details come from the trust documents themselves that were offered for auction on eBay.com. For the 1938 document, see seller "History for Sale" item number 372669390105 that was active on 13 Oct 2019. For the 1930 document, see the same seller item number 303185793612 that was active on 13 Oct 2019. Hawkins (pg. 236, note #19) cites a trust document in the JFK Library from Gus to this same bank, suggesting it was Pauline's $60K trust fund. Dearborn's biography suggests that Pauline had an income of $6,000 per year/$500 per month from her trust(s). This number is higher than that documented in Hawkins (pg. 47) and therefore likely includes the additional trusts created by Uncle Gus after their marriage. Yet, the source given by Dearborn for Pfeiffer wealth is Hawkins (pg. 13), which confirms that wealth exists but I could not find support for the specific number. It may be buried elsewhere in the text, notes, or afterward.
30. Baker 1969, 191
31. Baker 1969, 191
32. See "The Legend," The Ernest Hemingway Home and Museum. Posted: n.d. Accessed: 13 Oct 2019. https://www.hemingway-home.com/general/
33. Baker 1969, 221
34. Baker 1969, 225
35. Hendrickson 157
36. Hendrickson 157
37. Baker 1969, 226; Paul Hendrickson places the total closer to $30,000. (Hendrickson 30); Noble 92 and Hendrickson both share details of the financing.
38. Baker 1969, 210
39. Hawkins 178
40. Hawkins 200
41. Hawkins 200-201
42. Hawkins 213
43. Hawkins 213
44. cited in Hawkins 72
45. Dearborn 254-255
46. Hawkins 91
47. Hawkins 90

48. Hawkins 91
49. Hawkins 93; Dearborn 257
50. Hawkins 92
51. Hawkins 223
52. G. Hemingway 6-7.
53. Hawkins 269
54. Carlos Baker (1969) notes times when Pauline exhibited emotional problems that would manifest later in her life.
55. Hawkins 269
56. Hawkins 270
57. Hawkins 271
58. Hawkins 271
59. Hawkins 271
60. Hawkins 272
61. G. Hemingway 8-9
62. Baker 1969, 297
63. Baker 1969, 297

Chapter 4 - The Gellhorn Family

1. Rollyson 1990, 91
2. Rollyson 1990, 91
3. Rollyson 1990, 92
4. Rollyson 1990, 93; Baker 1969, 299
5. Rollyson 1990, 93
6. Baker 1969 298-299
7. Baker 1969 322
8. "Love Collaborates..." pp. 6-7
9. "Miss Gelhorn..." 1A
10. Moorehead 16
11. Moorehead 22
12. Rollyson 2001, 7

13. Rollyson 2001, 10
14. Rollyson 2001, 10
15. Moorehead 20, 25, 27
16. Moorehead 51
17. Moorehead 66
18. Rollyson 2001, 257-258
19. Rollyson 2001, 45
20. Rollyson 2001 50-51
21. Rollyson 2001, 51
22. Rollyson 2001, 51
23. Rollyson 2001, 54; The timeline given by Rollyson on pp. 51-54 is somewhat confusing; he seems to suggest that the love affair between Wells and Gellhorn "resumed" in January 1936, when he also suggests that the February 1936 letter to Eleanor for help started it in June of 1936. In telling this story, there are references to 1935. Obviously, a date is off by one year somewhere. The sourcing is unclear for this, and the facts are not readily available to clarify. The timing is especially challenging considering she had a 1936 affair with Allen Grover as well, all before meeting Ernest in December of that year.
24. Rollyson 2001, 55
25. Rollyson 2001 56-57
26. "Allen Grover, ex-Executive for Time Inc.," St. Louis Post Dispatch. 06 May 1993. 4C.
27. Moorehead 118
28. Rollyson 1990, 96
29. Baker 1969 304
30. Baker 1969 309
31. Baker 1969, 314-315
32. Baker 1969, 324
33. Baker 1969, 324
34. Baker 1969, 338
35. Rollyson 1990, 138-139
36. Rollyson 1990, 138
37. Rollyson 1990, 138

38. Rollyson 1990, 139
39. Rollyson 139-140
40. Rollyson 1990, 140
41. Rollyson 1990, 152
42. Rollyson 1990, 152
43. Rollyson 1990, 153
44. Rollyson 1990, 156
45. Moorhead 206
46. Rollyson 1990, 156
47. Moorhead 206
48. Baker 1969 351
49. Rollyson 1990, 157
50. Rollyson 1990, 156
51. Baker 1969 355-356
52. Rollyson 1990, 170
53. Rollyson 1990, 170
54. Rollyson 1990, 170
55. Rollyson 1990, 172
56. Rollyson 1990, 174
57. Baker 1969, 386
58. Baker 1996, 386
59. Baker 1996, 386-8
60. Baker 1996, 389
61. Baker 1996, 389
62. Baker 1996, 391. See the intriguing book Hemingway's Brain by Dr. Andrew Farah (University of South Carolina Press, 2017) that speaks in part to Hemingway's head trauma and the likely misdiagnosis of his troubles. [It has not risen to the top of my reading stack yet, but it's certainly in there.]
63. Baker 1969, 393
64. Baker 1969, 393
65. Baker 1969, 393
66. Baker 1969, 393-394
67. Baker 1996, 394-395

68. Baker 1996, 395
69. Baker 1996, 402
70. Baker 1996, 402-403
71. Baker 1996, 417-418
72. Baker 1996, 440; she had confided to her mother during a July 1945 visit that her marriage was ending (see "Martha Gellhorn Hemingway Sued by Author for Divorce," St. Louis Post-Dispatch, 21 Nov 1945, p. 3A).
73. Baker 1996, 441
74. Baker 1996, 443
75. Rollyson 2001, 164, 169
76. Rollyson 2001, 173-174; Rollyson 1990, 207
77. Baker 1969, 452
78. Baker 1969, 452

Chapter 5 - A. E. Hotchner and an Essay on Sources

1. Hotchner 4
2. Hotchner 7
3. Hotchner 7
4. Hotchner 267
5. Hotchner 268-9
6. Hotchner 288
7. Hotchner 289
8. Hotchner 291-293
9. Hotchner 297
10. Hotcher 302-303
11. "'Hemingway in Love' Chronicles Papa's Romantic Regrets," All Things Considered. Posted: 27 Oct 2015. Accessed: 24 Aug 2019. https://www.npr.org/2015/10/27/452311131/hemingway-in-love-chronicles-papas-romantic-regrets
12. Hotchner 304

13. See "Objects to a Book," The Kansas City Times. 15 Jan 1966. Pg. 2.

14. Hendrickson 126

15. Hendrickson 127

16. Hendrickson 122-123

17. See the St. John interview.

Bibliography

(Websites are noted in the endnotes for each chapter)

Baker, Carlos. (1969) *Ernest Hemingway: A Life Story.* New York: Macmillan, 1969.

Baker, Carlos. (1963) *Hemingway: The Writer as Artist.* 3rd ed. Princeton: Princeton University Press, 1963.

Blume, Lesley M. M. *Everybody Behaves Badly: The True Story behind Hemingway's Masterpiece* The Sun Also Rises. New York: Houghton Mifflin Harcourt, 2016.

Brian, Denis. *The True Gen.* New York: Delta, 1988.

Browne, Warren. *Titan Vs. Taboo: The Life of William Benjamin Smith.* Tucson, AZ: Diogenes, 1961.

Cappel (Montgomery), Constance. *Hemingway in Michigan.* Waitsfield VT: Vermont Crossroads Press, 1977.

Dearborn, Mary V. *Ernest Hemingway: A Biography.* New York: Alfred Knopf, 2017.

Diliberto, Gioia. (1992) *Hadley.* New York: Ticknor and Fields, 1992.

Diliberto, Gioia. (2011) *Paris without End: The True Story of Hemingway's First Wife.* New York: Harper Perennial, 1992/2011.

Donaldson, Scott. *By Force of Will: The Life and Art of Ernest Hemingway.* New York: Viking Press, 1977.

Fenton, Charles A. *The Apprenticeship of Ernest Hemingway.* Paperback ed. London: Plantin Publishers, (1954) 1987.

Frantz, Sali. *The Belvedere Club, Charlevoix, Michigan: Memoirs of Members 1878-1968.* Saginaw, MI: Seemann and Peters, Inc., 1969.

"Good Girl Gone Bad," *Chicago Tribune.* Posted: 02 Apr 2013. Accessed: 24 Aug 2019. <http://galleries.apps.chicagotribune.com/chi-130409-wanda-stopa-pictures/>

Gould's St. Louis Directory 1915. St. Louis: Gould Directory Co., 1915.

Gould's St. Louis Directory 1920. Vol. XLIX. St. Louis: Polk-Gould Directory Co., 1920.

Gould's St. Louis Directory 1921. Vol. L. St. Louis: Polk-Gould Directory Co., 1921.

Griffin, Peter. *Along with Youth: Hemingway, the Early Years*. New York: Oxford University Press, 1985.

Hawkins, Ruth A. *Unbelievable Happiness and Final Sorrow: The Hemingway- Pfeiffer Marriage*. Fayetteville AK: University of Arkansas Press, 2012.

Hemingway, Gregory. *Papa: A Personal Memoir*. Boston: Houghton Mifflin, 1976.

Hendrickson, Paul. *Hemingway's Boat: Everything He Loved in Life and Lost, 1934-1961*. New York: Alfred A. Knopf, 2011.

Hotchner, A. E. *Papa Hemingway: A Personal Memoir*. New York: Random House, 1966.

Johnston, Kenneth G. *The Tip of the Iceberg: Hemingway and the Short Story*. Greenwood FL: Penkevill Publishing Company, 1987.

Koontz, Leah Rice. "My Favorite Subject is Hadley," *The Connecticut Review*. 8:1, 36-41. October 1974.

Laymon, Sherry. *Pfeiffer Country: The Tenant Farms and Business Activities of Paul Pfeiffer in Clay County, Arkansas, 1902-1954*. Little Rock: Butler Center Books, 2009.

Leland, John. *A Guide to Hemingway's Paris*. Chapel Hill: Algonquin Books, 1989.

"Love Collaborates with Hemingway," *New York Daily News*. 08 Dec 1940 pp, 6-7.

Lynn, Kenneth. *Hemingway*. New York: Simon and Schuster, 1987.

Mellow, James R. *Hemingway: A Life without Consequences*. New York: Houghton Mifflin, 1992.

"Miss Gellhorn in Talk Here," *Des Moines Register*. 20 Jan 1938. 1A.

Moorehead, Caroline. *Martha Gellhorn: A Life*. New York: Vantage 2004 (2003).

Reynolds, Michael. (1986) *The Young Hemingway*. New York: Norton, 1998 (1986).

Reynolds, Michael. (1989) *Hemingway: The Paris Years*. New York: Norton, 1999 (1989).

Rintoul, M. C. *Dictionary of Real People and Places in Fiction.* New York: Routledge, 1993.

Rollyson, Carl. (2001) *Beautiful Exile: The Life of Martha Gellhorn.* London: Aurum Press, 2002 (2001).

Rollyson, Carl. (1990) *Nothing Ever Happens to the Brave: The Story of Martha Gellhorn.* New York: St. Martin's Press, 1990.

Smith, Marion Hammett. "Recollections of Dos," *Connecticut Review.* 8:2, 21-24. April 1975.

St. John, Donald. "Interview with Hemingway's 'Bill Gorton,'" *Hemingway and* The Sun *Set.* Bertram D. Sarason, ed. Washington: NCR Microcard Editions, 1972.

Severance, Henry Ormal. "William Benjamin Smith, Ph.D., LL.D., A Friend of the University of Missouri Library," *The University of Missouri Bulletin.* Vol. 37, No. 3, Series 17. Columbia MO: University of Missouri, 1936.

Sokoloff, Alice Hunt. *Hadley: The First Mrs. Hemingway.* New York: Dodd Mead, 1973.

Swisher, Walter Samuel. *A History of the Church of the Messiah: 1834-1934.* St. Louis: privately published. 1934.

Voss, Frederick. *Picturing Hemingway: A Writer in His Time.* New Haven: Yale University Press, 1999.

"Wandering Wanda," *Chicago Tribune.* 12 Jan 1947. Magazine pg. 26 (film page 77).

Acknowledgements

I am a scholar of cities and not of literature. I have stepped outside of my traditional academic boundaries in order to link two personal passions in a scholarly way—the history of St. Louis and the life of Ernest Hemingway. I am grateful to the many scholars of history and literature who have laid a strong foundation on which I could build this study. I have high respect for your work, which I hope is evident herein, and I hope that you do not consider this monograph an intrusion into your field but rather a unique expression of what your work has made possible.

I enjoy the support of many people, personally and professionally. It is their support that allows me to pursue interesting projects like this one. I am grateful to them all, and will attempt to name some of them here, with apologies for any omissions.

In 2013, I had the great pleasure of being part of a faculty exchange with the University of Havana. Somehow, somewhere, my university had one of the few open travel permits to Cuba from the 1960s, so the travel restrictions of the day did not apply in the same way. I'm grateful to Southern Illinois University for sponsoring such exchanges. The Dean of Arts and Sciences at the time was **Aldemaro Romero Jr**., who facilitated faculty and student travel through the Cuba and Caribbean Center initiative. **Dr. Larry Lafond** and **Dr. Wendy Shaw** were the trip leaders. It was Larry's fluency in Spanish that allowed me to arrange the driver for a side-trip to Finca Vigia. The Initiative for Urban Research funded my travel, and I'm grateful to the staff there: **Hugh Pavitt, Rhonda Penelton, Carrie Smolar, Julie Tucker Eudy**, and

Heather Birdsell. Dr. Jerry Weinberg was the dean and associate provost who supported the IUR at that time. My scholarly work in Cuba was to be shared with **Dr. Don Phares** from the University of Missouri, whose health prevented him from participating in the planned trip and who passed away thereafter.

In 2019-20, I still enjoyed the University's support. **Dr. Greg Budzban**, as Dean of Arts and Sciences, gave meaningful backing for the IUR. **Dr. Ken Moffett**, chair of the Political Science Department, as well as **Tara Huntley** who makes the department run smoothly, provided real support for this research project. I am thankful for such good colleagues. The sale of this book in part benefits the Initiative for Urban Research through the SIUE Foundation.

I am thankful for the support I received from Hemingway-focused institutions. **Maryrose Grossman** at the John F. Kennedy Library was very helpful in securing those early St. Louis-related photos—including the cover image. **Adam Long** at the Hemingway-Pfeiffer Museum was also very helpful and provided a needed image. **Keith Strom** of the Hemingway Foundation of Oak Park and **Leigh Tarullo** of the Oak Park Public Library helped secure permissions for electronic images. I'm grateful to all of these institutions for being good stewards of Hemingway's legacy. The secretaries of state in Missouri and Illinois both have cooperated in the digitization of their respective archival records and these files were immensely helpful in the research and production of this book. Thank you to both of these offices. I am also grateful to the Merrill family descendants, especially **Jim Durand**, for sharing the family archives that had been shared by earlier generations for the Browne and Carr books.

I wish to single-out and honor **Clive Baugh**'s website, *clive-w.blogspot.com*, for his outstanding tour of Hemingway sites in northern Michigan. I've never met or contacted him but I thoroughly enjoyed seeing his photos of some of the sites described in the first chapter of this monograph. His work is solid and reliable, and presented in a fun and accessible manner. I'm glad to see the Michigan sites that embrace their Hemingway heritage. I look forward to making a trip!

Acknowledgements

It was a great pleasure for me to meet **Bruce R. Olson** during this work. Bruce spent much of his career as a writer and editor for Reuters, and is an outstanding researcher. If you have never examined his *That St. Louis Thing* volumes, then I recommend you do. I was so impressed with the Hemingway portions of his book that I had to meet him. Bruce believed in the merits of this project and provided much-needed editorial support. **Dallas T. Moses** (designer extraordinaire) and **David LaGesse** and **Laura Stanton** (publishers extraordinaire) provided critical technical support.

Additionally, I'm grateful for the people in my closest circle who have lent their talents to answer my questions, explain complex processes, and offer insight from their years of wisdom. I often turn to my partner, **Dr. Alexis Elward**, for advice. She is Professor of Pediatric Infectious Diseases at the Washington University School of Medicine. She is a national expert in infectious disease and she helped me interpret death certificates, newspaper articles, and answered all my medical questions about the subjects of this book (a surprising number of whom died of infection). My son **Evan Theising** has provided feedback, insight, and patience for yet another book project. **Dr. Larry Eisenman**, friend and neurologist, took time to explain to me what Hemingway's electro-shock therapy would have been like, the medical goals of such procedures, and the lingering effects of it. I'm very grateful to my sister-in-law **Susan Andrews** ("Hemingway-Schwemingway") who, along with her son **Jack**, read manuscripts, offered editorial comments, provided cover design feedback, and helped make content decisions.

I value my colleagues who enable good work and **I value you** who read this work. Your feedback and corrections are welcome. You can reach me through Southern Illinois University Edwardsville, *www.siue.edu*. All errors herein are mine. I apologize in advance for them and am grateful for your corrections and additions.

Dr. Andrew J. Theising
Webster Groves, Mo

Index

c = caption, n = note

Allan-Pfeiffer Chemical Co. facing i, 60, 128 n13

Ambos Mundos Hotel 85

Anderson, Sherwood 21, 26, 48, 118 n34, 120 n72 n73

Archera, Laura (Huxley) 71, 72

Baker, Carlos 8, 10c, 30c, 42, 54, 58, 64, 77, 104-105, 110, 117 n25, 121 n74, 126 n70, 130 n54

Belvedere Hotel (Charlevoix) 5, 117 n20

Bird, Bill 84

Bradfield, Ruth 33, 34, 36, 48, 123 n10

Breaker, George J. facing i, 32, 33, 34, 35, 46-47, 48, 50, 51, 52-53, 99

Breaker, Helen Pierce facing i, 32, 33, 34, 35, 44, 45, 48, 50, 52, 53, 99, 114, 123 n10, 125 n67

Brian, Denis 99, 112

Cape Cod, MA 9, 11, 27, 122 n99

Charles, Rev. Benjamin Hynes 6, 22

Charles Farm 11, 12, 13, 15, 18, 24, 25, 27, 44, 117 n25

Charles, Dr. Joseph W. "Unk" 1, 6, 12, 17, 21-22, 23, 48, 117 n23 n25, 121 n86,

Charles, Laura Merrill "Aunty" facing i, iv, 1, 2, 3, 4, 6, 9, 11, 12c, 24, 25, 27, 28, 32, 33, 34, 35, 36, 44, 45, 48, 49, 50, 51, 64, 72, 99, 100c, 117 n25

Charlevoix Home Association 5, 6

Charlevoix, MI 5, 6, 12c, 25, 51

Charlevoix Lake 5, 6, 7, 12, 13, 15, 25, 44

Cheyenne, WY 88

Clemens, Cyril 67

Colette 79

D-Day 93, 94

Dearborn, Mary V. 8, 97, 112, 117-118 n29, 120 n73, 122 n99,125 n67, 128 n18 n26, 129 n29

Diliberto, Gioia 33, 37, 40, 42, 108, 117 n25, 122 n7, 123 n9 n10 n27, 124 n33 n43, 125 n56, 126 n70 n77, 127 n82

Dilworth Inn/Cottages 12, 13, 15, 24, 44, 117 n25

Donaldson, Scott 1, 110, 111

Dos Passos, John 10, 11, 18, 21, 27, 69

East St. Louis, IL 2, 16, 115 n1 n4, 116 n6 n17

Edgar, J. Charles "Carl" 7, 8c, 11, 28c, 47c, 110

Eliot, T.S. i, 1, 49

Eliot, William Greenleaf 1, 4

Elward, Alexis 141

Fenton, Charles 109

Finca Vigia ii, 75, 83, 86, 89, 90c, 91, 101, 139

Florissant, MO 78

Foley, Edith (Shay) 9, 20, 26, 122 n99

Foster, Gilbert B. 2, 4, 11

Gellhorn, Edna Fischel 72, 75, 76, 77-78, 79, 80, 81, 86-87, 88, 101

Gellhorn, George 42, 77, 78, 81, 82c

Gellhorn, Martha (third wife) ii, iii, 42, 72, 74c, 75-97, 99, 101, 108-109, 111, 114, 131 n23, 133 n72

Given, Eben 11

Griffin, Peter 19, 32, 43c, 110-111, 117 n26, 121 n86, 123 n11 n12, 124 n51, 125 n61 n67, 126 n77 n81

Grover, Allen 82-83, 131 n23

Hammett, Marion (Smith) 10, 18, 122 n99
Hawkins, Ruth 63c, 69, 108, 128 n26, 129 n29
Havana, Cuba 65, 85, 86, 90c, 91, 100, 101, 112, 139
Hemingway, Ernest
    in Chicago 9, 20, 24, 26, 28c, 35, 54
    in Cuba 65, 85-87, 89, 90-91, 100-101
    in Key West 65, 66, 68, 70c, 72, 75, 76, 84
    Marriages iii, 44, 58, 88, 96
    in Michigan 7, 9, 13, 16, 24, 25, 44, 46-47, 48
    in Paris 48-49, 54, 57-58, 65
    in St. Louis 17c, 33, 34, 78c, 101
    in World War I 24, 28c
    in World War II 90-97
Hemingway, Clarence 7, 35, 43, 46c, 68, 69, 114
Hemingway, Grace Hall 7, 28c, 35, 43, 88, 89, 91, 96
Hemingway, Gregory "Gigi" 59, 69, 70-72, 89, 107, 114
Hemingway, John "Jack" "Bumby" 49, 107
Hemingway, Leicester 86, 107, 114
Hemingway, Madelaine "Sunny" (Miller) 28c, 64, 107
Hemingway, Marcelline (Sanford) 8c, 28c, 106
Hemingway, Patrick 58, 65, 68, 69, 70c, 72, 107-108, 127 n7
Hemingway, Ursula 28c, 114, 125 n67
Hendrickson, Paul 110, 111-112, 129 n37,
Hopkins, Charles H. 28c, 46-47
Horne, William D. "Bill" 8c, 26, 27, 31, 34, 41, 46-47, 48, 110, 125 n67
Horton Bay, MI 6, 7c, 9, 11-13, 15, 19, 24, 25, 27, 43, 44, 45c, 46, 48, 51, 119 n49, 120 n66
Hotchner, A.E. ii, 97, 98, 99-104, 105, 16, 107, 108
Hudnut, Richard Company 61c, 62

Jenkins, Howell 11, 46-47
Jouvenel, Bertrand de 77, 79-80, 81

Kert, Bernice G. 109

Key West, FL 10c, 59c, 65, 66, 67, 68, 69, 70c, 71, 75, 76, 82c, 83, 84, 85, 110

Kirkwood, MO 67

Knox, Isaac 2

Lanham, Charles T. "Buck" 94-95, 96

Loeb, Harold 18, 57

London, England 91-92, 94, 95, 96

Longfield Farm 24, 25

Louisiana, MO 4, 5, 11, 15, 24, 27c

Lynn, Kenneth S. 111, 125 n67

MacLeish, Archibald 66-67

Mellow, James R. 15, 111, 120 n72 n73, 125 n67

Merrill, Leonard 2, 50, 72

Merrill, Kathleen "Kate" (Smith) ivc, 1, 2-5, 7,11, 13, 114, 116 n8 n17, 117 n20

Meyers, Jeffrey 111

Monks, Noel 91, 95

Nagel, James 112

Nast, Conde 62, 128 n19

Pailthorp, Edwin "Dutch" 46-47, 48

Petoskey, MI 6, 12, 25, 45c, 46-47, 69

Pfeiffer Chemical Company ii, 61, 62, 68

Pfeiffer, Gustavus A. "Uncle Gus" facing i, ii, 57, 59, 61, 62, 63, 64-68, 72, 129 n29

Pfeiffer, Henry 59, 60, 61, 62, 64

Pfeiffer, Mary 61, 62, 63, 64

Pfeiffer, Paul 61, 62, 63, 64, 69

Pfeiffer, Pauline (second wife) facing i, ii, iii, 10-11, 35, 56c, 57-59, 61, 62-72, 76-77, 84, 85, 86, 87, 88, 96, 108, 114, 129 n29, 130 n54

Pfeiffer, Virginia "Jinny" 57, 71, 72

Pierce, Lawrence and Lucie 51

Piggott, AR 62, 64, 68-69, 71

Pilar ii, 101, 112,

Polk, William Julius 78

Reynolds, Michael 110, 111, 126 n70

Richardson, Clifford 37, 39

Richardson Drug Company facing i, ii, 31, 36, 37, 38, 39, 60

Richardson, Florence Wyman 31, 36-38, 40, 41, 42, 43, 53, 126 n75

Richardson, Hadley (first wife) facing i, ii, iii, 1, 10, 11, 16, 19c, 20, 21, 26-27, 28, 29c, 31-45, 48-55, 57-58, 63, 64, 66, 77, 78, 79, 84, 87, 96, 108, 114, 121 n74, 124 n43, 125 n61 n 67, 126 n70 n75

Richardson, James facing i, 31, 36-37, 38, 39

Rollyson, Carl 91, 109, 131 n23

Roosevelt, Eleanor 81, 82, 87, 99, 131 n23

Samuelson, Arnold 109-110

Smith, Blanche Genevieve Dawley "Doodles" 19, 20, 21, 26,

Smith, Jennie Drake 4

Smith, Katharine Foster "Katy" ii, facing 1, 1, 2-3, 4, 6, 7-11, 14c, 15, 16, 18, 19, 20, 21, 24, 26, 27, 28, 31, 32, 44, 48, 62, 65, 69, 78, 114, 115 n1, 117 n21, 117-118 n29, 118 n34, 120 n71, 122 n99

Smith, Merrill facing 1, 3, 6, 12c, 23, 24, 114, 117 n21

Smith, William Benjamin Jr. "Bill" ii, facing 1, 3, 4, 5, 6, 7, 8c, 9, 10, 11, 12c, 14, 15, 16-18, 19, 21-22, 24, 26, 27, 28-29, 42, 46-47, 48, 57, 69, 110, 113, 115 n1, 116 n17, 119 n54 n56, 120 n71, 122 n99, 125 n67

Smith, William Benjamin Sr. 2-3, 6, 13-15, 116 n8, 118 n45, 119 n49 n53

Smith, Yeremyah Kenley "Y.K." facing 1, 3, 6, 11, 15, 18-21, 26, 28, 35, 44, 48, 57, 117 n21, 118 n74 n83, 119 n49, 120 n70 n71 n72 n73, 121 n74 n83

Smooley Hall 9, 27, 122 n99

Sokoloff, Alice Hunt 31, 48, 108, 125 n67, 127 n82

Stopa, Wanda E. 20-21, 114, 121 n79

Sun Valley, ID 87

Taille de Noyer 78

Thompson, Charles 67, 68, 76

Usher, Florence "Fonchen" (Lord) 41, 42, 43, 124 n47

Usher, Florence "Fonnie" facing i, 31, 32, 33, 34, 38, 40-43, 44, 48, 124 n43 n51

Usher, Roland Greene 33, 40c, 41, 42, 44

Walloon Lake 7, 12, 13,

Warner, William R. Company 61c, 62, 65, 128 n18

Washington University in St. Louis 1, 23, 41, 75, 100, 101, 141

Webster Groves, MO 36, 38, 67, 141

Wells, H. G. 81, 82, 89, 131 n23

Welsh, Mary (fourth wife) iii, 91, 92, 93, 94, 95, 96, 102-104, 105-106, 109

White, Trumbull i

Windemere Cottage 7, 13, 25, 44, 69

Wright, Don 20, 110

Wyman, Arthur 36, 127 n82

Wyman, Charles 36

Wyman, Frank 36, 49, 53, 127 n82

Wyman, Henry 36

Wyman, Walter 36

Made in USA - Kendallville, IN
1186674_9781950419067
10 27 2020 1050